THE POWER OF
INVISIBLE
LEADERSHIP

To grandson, Ryan Pitcher, with my deepest hope that you will find the passion and commitment of invisible leadership in your life.

And

To daughter and friend, Suzanna Strasburg Fitzpatrick, a joy to all.

THE POWER OF
INVISIBLE
LEADERSHIP

How a Compelling Common Purpose
Inspires Exceptional Leadership

Gill Robinson Hickman
University of Richmond

Georgia J. Sorenson
University of Maryland

Los Angeles | London | New Delhi
Singapore | Washington DC

Los Angeles | London | New Delhi
Singapore | Washington DC

FOR INFORMATION:

SAGE Publications, Inc.

2455 Teller Road

Thousand Oaks, California 91320

E-mail: order@sagepub.com

SAGE Publications Ltd.

1 Oliver's Yard

55 City Road

London, EC1Y 1SP

United Kingdom

SAGE Publications India Pvt. Ltd.

B 1/I 1 Mohan Cooperative Industrial Area

Mathura Road, New Delhi 110 044

India

SAGE Publications Asia-Pacific Pte. Ltd.

3 Church Street

#10-04 Samsung Hub

Singapore 049483

Acquisitions Editor: Patricia Quinlin

Editorial Assistant: Katie Guarino

Production Editor: Stephanie Palermini

Copy Editor: Cate Huisman

Typesetter: Hurix Systems Pvt. Ltd.

Proofreader: Talia Greenberg

Indexer: Karen Wiley

Cover Designer: Gail Buschman

Marketing Manager: Liz Thornton

Permissions Editor: Adele Hutchinson

Printed in the United States of America.

Library of Congress Cataloging-in-Publication Data

Hickman, Gill Robinson.

The power of invisible leadership : how a compelling common purpose inspires exceptional leadership / Gill Robinson Hickman, University of Richmond, Georgia J. Sorenson, University of Maryland.

pages cm

Includes bibliographical references and index.

ISBN 978-1-4129-4017-7 (pbk. : alk. paper)

1. Leadership. I. Sorenson, Georgia J. II. Title.

HD57.7.H5223 2013

658.4'092—dc23

2012039560

This book is printed on acid-free paper.

13 14 15 16 17 10 9 8 7 6 5 4 3 2 1

Brief Contents

Detailed Contents

Acknowledgments

W e spent many years developing ideas and testing pertinent concepts for this book with various audiences, colleagues, and organizations. Our sincere and heartfelt thanks go to each of you for your contributions, support, and encouragement.

We are forever indebted to James MacGregor Burns for bringing the two of us together to become lifelong friends and colleagues—just as he knew we would. We are especially grateful to Tammy Tripp, coordinator of communications and academic research at the Jepson School of Leadership Studies, for her expert editing, her persistent requests for permissions and information, and her wonderful disposition and patience. We also want to thank Cassie Price, who edited our initial paper on invisible leadership.

Writing this book would not have been possible without the special support and expertise of Traci Fenton, founder and CEO of WorldBlu, and Harvey Seifter, director and principal investigator at The Art of Science Learning and president of Seifter Associates. We are infinitely grateful for the time and contributions of our survey participants, who are from organizations currently or previously on the WorldBlu List of Most Democratic Workplaces, including AIESEC International, Axiom News, BetterWorld Telecom, Brainpark, Chroma Technology, Dialog Group, Dreamhost, Equal Exchange, Future Considerations, Glassdoor.com, Haiti Partners, ILoveRewards, Innovation Partners International, Menlo Innovations, Mindvalley, Nearsoft, NixonMcInnes, Rypple, sweetriot, TakingITGlobal, and UniversalGiving.

We especially want to thank our faculty colleagues at the Jepson School—Don Forsyth for graciously contributing his expertise in statistical analysis for our preliminary and final surveys, and Crystal Hoyt for her help with conceptualization, hypothesis development, and analysis. Thank you to Terry Price for his contributions to our discussion of the ethics of invisible leadership. The three of you gave so selflessly of your time and expertise to this project. You supported us to the very end, and we are truly appreciative.

Early and dedicated readers and supporters include Francie Glendening, Jean Lipman-Blumen, David Gergen, Krish Raval, Bruce Avolio, and Deborah Meehan.

Many students at the Jepson School contributed to the early development of concepts and survey questions for this project. We wish to thank our students in the Senior Seminar on Invisible Leadership for strengthening the conceptual elements in our theory—Devron Allen, Evan Baum, Christa Chamberlain, Kelly Decker, Cammy Desmond, Will Gooding, Sara Hormell, Janelle Hubert, Nathan Marconi, Patricia North, Laura Pendleton, Kristen Peterson, Katherine Ponzio, Liz Rupp, Amy Scalia, Danny Silver, Katie Sloan, Jonathan Stells, and Benjamin Tengwall. We are also appreciative of the insights on invisible leadership from students in the Theories and Models of Leadership classes and for their input on the survey questions.

Participants at several International Leadership Association annual conferences played a vital role in the development of our ideas. We especially want to thank attendees at the session and roundtable discussion of invisible leadership and those who have adopted our model in research activities. Your comments, advice, and work helped us immeasurably.

We are thankful to the editors and staff of SAGE Publications for their expertise and support during the editing and publication of the book, especially Patricia Quinlin, Katie Guarino, Lisa Shaw, MaryAnn Vail, the late Al Bruckner, Laureen Gleason, and Stephanie Palermini. The authors and SAGE Publications would like to thank the following reviewers for their wisdom and advice: Alison L. Antes, PhD, Northern Kentucky University; Frederick Brockmeier, JD, PhD, Northern Kentucky University; Ginny Russell Curley, PhD, Nebraska Methodist College; Douglas Davenport, PhD, Truman State University; Rosa A. Gonzalez, PhD, SUNY Erie Community College; Bryan Patterson, PhD, Johnson C. Smith University; and Angela Nicole Scott, PhD, Lehigh University.

On a personal note, we would like to thank our family and friends for their love and support during the course of our work on this project. We would like to express our deepest gratitude to Gill's husband, Garrison Michael Hickman, for his supportive and loving care throughout the preparation of this book. He made every sacrifice to ensure that we were able to bring this book to fruition. Ms. Punky and Mr. Brewster played their own invisible role in supporting the work, but Michael deserves our deepest appreciation.

1

Unmasking Leadership

This book explores the idea of invisible leadership—leadership in which the common purpose, rather than any particular individual, is the invisible leader that inspires leaders and followers to take action on its behalf. It is an idea that often goes unrecognized in the study and practice of leadership. We will examine stories and organizations where invisible leadership propels groups to the highest levels of commitment, innovation, and success. We will also provide evidence of the power of invisible leadership in action.

What we will describe exists in the space between people and in their shared dreams. Although that space is completely invisible, the effect is immensely powerful. We have called this region "the space between" and compared it to American jazz great Thelonious Monk's "blue notes." An evening spent listening to Monk's jazz saxophone on "Straight, No Chaser" is an experience you will never forget. But why is his music so extraordinary? Jazz critics attribute the genius of Monk's remarkable musical gift to the nuance, phrasing, and rhythm of the spaces between the formal notes. Indeed, it is the relationship between notes that makes the music soar, not the actual notes themselves. The score shows you the formal notes, not the blue notes, yet it is the blue notes in the performance that stir your soul and transform the musical experience.

Note: We presented portions of this chapter at the China Executive Leadership Academy Pudong Leadership Conference, October 19–20, 2007, in Shanghai, China. We also presented some of these concepts in these publications:

Hickman, G. R. (2004). Invisible leadership. In G. R. Goethals, G. Sorenson, & J. M. Burns (Eds.), *Encyclopedia of leadership* (pp. 750–754). Thousand Oaks, CA: Sage.

Sorenson, G., & Hickman, G. R. (2002). Invisible leadership: Acting on behalf of a common purpose. In C. Cherrey & L. R. Matusak (Eds.), *Building leadership bridges* (pp. 7–24). College Park, MD: James MacGregor Burns Academy of Leadership.

Although it is not readily apparent, there is a lot going on that we can't see, as can be discerned from a number of scientific lenses, from the cosmic to the intrapsychic. Note the recent findings of dark holes in the universe yielding a churning cauldron of organizing dark material. NASA recently confirmed what was speculation by Fritz Zwicky in the 1930s: "Most of the stuff in clusters of galaxies is invisible and, since these are the largest structures in the universe held together by gravity, scientists then conclude that most of the matter in the entire universe is invisible." This invisible "dark matter" is the rich "space between" of our cosmos (NASA, n.d.).

Noted psychoanalyst Harry Stack Sullivan revolutionized the practice of psychotherapy by working solely within the space between the patient and therapist. He reasoned that whatever the patient's dysfunction or unhappiness—a tragic childhood, a distant catastrophic event, a numbing malaise, or another disturbing event or condition—it would eventually show up in the developing relationship between the patient and therapist (Barton & Sullivan, 1996). The space was like a mirror to the past; if he remained still and listened carefully, the experience would be replicated in full in the space between him and the patient. He could then work backward toward the genesis of the original dysfunction. We can learn much in the space between ourselves and others and in our shared work toward an inspiring common purpose.

This invisible space, while subtle, is not inaccessible to us, however. Sometimes we sense it in music, such as Monk's work, or in great art. Take, for example, the extraordinary photographs that short-story writer Eudora Welty made when she was young. Just out of college, Welty was hired by Franklin D. Roosevelt's Works Progress Administration to travel her native state of Mississippi. She took along her camera to photograph the people she met on the road. In an undated photograph she titled "Saturday Off," the sense of intimacy and trust between the photograph's subject—a young Jackson, Mississippi, woman—and the photographer is profoundly evident. It is this utterly invisible human interaction that makes the photograph great.

Welty described her work this way: "In taking . . . these pictures, I was attended, I now know, by an angel—a presence of trust" (Pleasants, 2001). The trust is the blue note, the invisible space between, the relationship between the two women that makes this photograph extraordinary. Great art emerges in the space between, that inexplicable sense of connection that goes beyond the technical abilities of the artist.

Revealing the Hidden Leader—The Common Purpose

So what do the ideas of blue notes, unseen spaces, and the space between dark matter and people have to do with leadership, the subject of this book? We think it has everything to do with a concept we call *invisible*

Photo 1.1   "Saturday Off," from the Eudora Welty Collection.

Source: Reprinted courtesy of the Eudora Welty Collection, Mississippi Department of Archives and History, and Russell & Volkening as agents for the author's estate. Copyright ©1936 & 1971 Eudora Welty, LLC.

leadership. Invisible leadership embodies situations in which dedication to a compelling and deeply held common purpose is the motivating force for leadership. This common purpose provides inspiration for participants to use their strengths willingly in leader or follower roles and cultivates a strong shared bond that connects participants to each other in pursuit of their purpose.

As we will see in the results of our study of award-winning innovative companies and nonprofit organizations, passionate commitment to and ownership of the common purpose occur when participants join

> **Invisible leadership** embodies situations in which *dedication to a compelling and deeply held common purpose* is the motivating force for leadership.

together because the purpose embodies deeply meaningful shared experiences, beliefs, values, or goals. The commonality of participants' experiences, beliefs, or values moves them beyond self-interest to focus on the well-being of a group, organization, or society. Participants initiate leadership for a common purpose based on a perceived opportunity to act and on their individual or collective self-agency. Opportunity occurs when resources (human, monetary, intellectual, or social capital) become available, or when a precipitating event provides the catalyst for action. Participants rely on self-agency and collective efficacy to advance the purpose and create new approaches, power structures, or institutions, or to defy existing authorities and institutions that are unresponsive or unjust.

The purpose is more than a mission statement, as many respondents in our study confirmed. Common purpose is a deeply held sense of common destiny, a life course or calling; it is aligned with a mission but resonates profoundly with people's values and their sense of themselves. It is the substance that binds people together and the aim or reason for their collective leadership. We found that it is often the reason people are attracted to the work of a business, nonprofit, community initiative, or social movement. It is also the reason they stay. This invisible force becomes the space where inspiration, interactions, and connection between a purpose and its leaders and followers ignite to bring about something extraordinary. It is more powerful than the classic Weberian charismatic personality, because it goes beyond individuals and institutions. We call this charisma of purpose.

Think about the first time you read or saw *The Wizard of Oz*. At the end of the story, you were astonished by the man behind the curtain. He looked and sounded nothing like the larger-than-life image (the great leader) that awed and intimidated Dorothy and her friends.

The story teaches us much about the essence of invisible leadership. At first we are disappointed to see the small person behind the curtain. But Dorothy and her friends show us that there is nothing as motivating and powerful as an inspiring purpose. They need committed involvement with each other to find the wizard (the common purpose, in this case). They must be willing to play leader and follower roles at different times, and even make personal sacrifices to further the group's goals. One of the most important lessons that Dorothy and her friends learn is that they have the power or self-agency to achieve their cherished goal. While meeting their collective goal, the common purpose, each character gains something different and valuable from the experience. The Tin Man finds his heart, the Lion gains courage, the Scarecrow discovers his brain, and Dorothy finds that she has the power to return to her family in Kansas. They each develop a better and stronger self and form an enduring bond of relationship, leadership, and action in the invisible space between.

Can a common purpose actually inspire leadership? Our research leads us to believe that it can. When you ask most people about leadership, they think of extraordinary individuals—their abilities, experience, traits, circumstances, and situations. Many scholars and students of leadership studies are conditioned to think of leadership in terms of the leader (like the great and powerful wizard) helping a group of followers understand and commit to an important purpose, the leader influencing and persuading followers to do the work and reach the goal. In fact, a great deal of leadership is done this way or at least characterized this way. Our work, however, and the work of other leadership scholars described in Chapter 2, led us to consider other ways that leadership can occur. Invisible leadership does not eliminate leaders. It emphasizes the idea of leader-as-role over leader-as-person, as introduced in the work of organizational behaviorist Robert Kelley (1988, 1992). The use of leader-as-role allows for a more fluid and multifaceted process where responsibility can be distributed among multiple actors or concentrated in one person. The crucial role of leaders in invisible leadership, as we describe in Chapter 6, is to create a context or environment where invisible leadership can thrive and the common purpose flourishes as lived experience among participants.

We asked our colleagues and ourselves: Does leadership involve the same dynamic when people already understand and are committed to an important purpose? When they know what needs to be done and willingly bring their talents and skills to the work? When they hold themselves responsible and accountable for achieving the common purpose? When they sometimes put the purpose ahead of their personal needs or safety?

After some work in this realm, we discovered that the idea of a common purpose inspiring people to initiate leadership is not a new concept. Mary Parker Follett, an early management scholar and practitioner in the United States, first described this concept in 1928. Instead of the accepted or classical view of leadership as people following a charismatic leader, Follett observed that in certain highly effective companies, leaders and followers are both following the invisible leader—the common purpose:

> While leadership depends on depth of conviction and the power coming therefrom, there must also be the ability to share that conviction with others, the ability to make purpose articulate. And then the common purpose becomes the leader. And I believe that we are coming more and more to act, whatever our theories, on our faith in this power of this invisible leader. Loyalty to the invisible leader gives us the strongest possible bond of union. (Follett, 1949/1987, p. 55)

Invisible leadership takes into account the people and the processes of leadership but stretches beyond these parameters into a realm of leadership and action that encompasses wholeness of purpose and the transformation of people, wisdom and values within the group, ethics of the purpose, means and ends, and limitless possibilities. Thus, "increasing shareholder value" is not antithetical to a common purpose, as highly successful entrepreneur Béla Hatvany will later tell us. The purpose is the leader and motivating force for all aspects of the enterprise.

The Essence of Invisible Leadership

How did we happen upon this concept? We developed our initial conception of invisible leadership by analyzing situations where leadership appeared to be inspired by the purpose as much as or more than by the influence of particular leaders (Sorenson & Hickman, 2002). We probed case studies of business and nonprofit organizations; studied written accounts of social movements; and examined existing interviews with activists, initiators of change, entrepreneurs, and organizational founders. We examined how other fields (physics, psychology, management, music, and photography) and cultures (Asian, African, and Native American) use the idea of invisible processes. We also explored the concept with focus groups of leadership scholars, educators, and professionals in lectures and workshops, and engaged leadership studies students in a semester-long examination of the topic.

As we distilled our thinking, we settled on three essential points that are fundamental to invisible leadership, although there are numerous subsets of these points that we enumerate in our research design in Chapter 4:

- A compelling and deeply held common purpose,
- A readiness to use individual strengths in either leader or follower roles with or without visible recognition or personal ego, and
- A strong shared bond among participants pursuing the common purpose.

For this study, we surveyed 21 award-winning companies and nonprofit workplaces to test our concepts. The results are detailed in Chapters 4 and 5. We include the survey results in these chapters to encourage further research on invisible leadership. Indeed, our study is a starting point that we hope will lead to further scholarship on this topic.

Invisible Leadership in Action

People tell us they can easily see that compelling social causes with a common purpose, such as the civil rights movement or the environmental movement, can certainly inspire individuals to act collectively and bring about a common good. They are not convinced, however, that other contexts can generate such strong, committed leadership from most people in the process without one prominent leader motivating the group and showing the way. We believe that invisible leadership can and does exist in companies, governmental bodies, nonprofit organizations, neighborhoods, schools, communities, and grassroots and social movements. The examples that follow come from our examination of existing case studies of organizations; written accounts of social movements in autobiographies and biographies; and interviews with activists, initiators of change, and organizational founders (Sorenson & Hickman, 2002).

Illustrations From Nonprofit Organizations

In the nonprofit arena, the Orpheus Chamber Orchestra is a conductor-less ensemble founded on the belief that musicians can create extraordinary music when an orchestra uses the full talents and creativity of every member (Seifter & Economy, 2001). Its purpose is to demonstrate a collaborative leadership style in which the musicians, rather than a conductor, interpret the score. Leader and follower roles are fluid and rotating, permitting members of the ensemble to share equally in the group's leadership. All the while, the group's leadership remains invisible to the public. The driving force of the orchestra is its common purpose, as Seifter and Economy (2001) make clear:

> Above all, Orpheus Chamber Orchestra is marked by our passionate dedication to our mission. That passion drives every musical and business decision that we make. Our organization's mission isn't imposed from above but is determined—and constantly refined—by the members themselves. (p. 16)

We observed the Orpheus model personally in a demonstration with several of the Czech Republic's finest chamber orchestra musicians at the International Leadership Association in Prague several years ago. The concert was truly amazing. Fascinated, we later interviewed Harvey Seifter (2009), former executive director of the Orpheus Chamber Orchestra. We learned just how radical the Orpheus model truly is: There is no conductor! Members of the orchestra share and rotate leadership roles. As Seifter and Economy (2001) described in their book, for every work that they perform, orchestra members select the concertmaster and principal players for each section. These players constitute the core group, form initial concepts of the piece, and shape the rehearsal process. At final rehearsals, all members participate in refining, interpreting, and executing the piece. Members take turns listening from the auditorium for balance, blend, articulation, dynamic range, and clarity of expression and give feedback to the group.

Another example from the nonprofit sector is C-SPAN. Brian Lamb started C-SPAN to provide direct and unfiltered broadcasts of public policy matters to the American people so that they could decide key issues for themselves (Frantzich & Sullivan, 1996). Although he retains a powerful influence on C-SPAN, in the 34 years he has been broadcasting, Lamb has never spoken his own name on the air (Farhi, 2012). Lamb along with those who fund C-SPAN and the founding members of the organization believe wholeheartedly in its purpose and persevere in their quest to bring public issues to the people. C-SPAN's approach to reporting and media competition has been credited with "transforming American politics" (Hazlett, 1996). The broadcast has gained tremendous respect and popularity since its inception in 1975. Even so, Lamb, in keeping with the role and style of invisible leadership, was determined to have increasingly less influence on C-SPAN. At the same time, when we first interviewed him, Lamb (1999) saw no particular reason to prepare for organizational succession. When Lamb did make the transition in 2012, the succession was publicly seamless. "I never thought the person on top here mattered all that much, except to keep the rhythm of the place going," he said (Farhi, 2012).

Illustrations From Public Sector (Government) Organizations

Much of the leadership in public sector agencies below the political appointee level is, by design, invisible. At its best, invisible leadership in public agencies consists of men and women who work on behalf of the public good without particular recognition or fanfare. They are quite literally "public servants."

Invisible leadership is strongest in public sector agencies when organizational members regard citizens as their central focus, truly care about citizens' well-being, and gain their inspiration from the compelling common purpose of their agency. These "servants" serve the public first, and their commitment to serve is true in the United States and in other countries around the globe.

Accenture (2006) studied public leadership in 21 countries throughout Africa, Asia, Australia, Europe, North America, and South America and discovered that leadership in high-performing public sector agencies has a "citizens-first" point of view—all necessary information is organized around the citizen, and is particularly focused on their desired outcomes, which are defined by the mission (p. 1).

A nationwide, representative telephone survey of 1,051 U.S. federal government workers and 500 private sector employees, conducted by the

Princeton Survey Research Institute for political scientist Paul Light at the Brookings Institution, found federal workers were split in their motivation to join the public sector: Some joined for job security and others for their commitment to the mission of public service (typically the higher-level employees). The report concludes, "Whatever their primary motivation for coming to work each day, the key question for a healthy public service is whether employees care about their organizations' missions" (Light, 2001, p. 4).

Some tribal governments in the United States, such as the Cherokee Nation, have built their communities around purpose, mission, and service. Again, a leader whose personal style was consistent with these factors arose in the Cherokee Nation. Wilma Mankiller was the first woman to be elected chief of a major Native American tribe, which made her quite visible. Invisible leadership does not require leaders or followers to be invisible. It is the space between that is invisible—the strong bond of relationship and leadership generated by a group's shared work toward a compelling and deeply held common purpose.

Beginning with a small project—a 16-mile water line to rural homes— Mankiller turned the economy and the identity of the Cherokee Nation around. During Mankiller's term of office, the Cherokee Nation grew its net worth from $34.6 million to nearly $52 million. It funded $20 million in new construction, including job corps facilities, health clinics, an educational center, and a museum. Unemployment rates and high school dropout rates slowed dramatically, even in the face of slashed federal programs for Native Americans during the Reagan years.

What was her secret? She was a true follower of the invisible leader—the common purpose of the Cherokee Nation. Mankiller never lost this focus. Her cultural identity is central in her sense of self and purpose, she told us:

> Knowing and valuing our culture helps me keep some perspective and keeps my feet on the ground. I have to spend so much time away from the basic kind of work I started out doing, which is community organizing and Indian advocacy. Now much of my work is involved in administration, lobbying in Washington, activities of that nature. It's still development, but it's at a different level. To keep my feet on the ground, I still participate in tribal ceremonies and make sure I take the time to be involved in Cherokee culture, even if it's much less time than I'd like. I still do that because it keeps things in perspective. There is something very grounding about going to a tribal ceremony that has been celebrated since time immemorial—to sing songs and participate in dances that we have been doing forever. That's the anchor. (Mankiller, 1992)

Although Mankiller is frequently described as a visionary, she is a visionary who is very aggressive about achieving the goals she has in mind for her people, goals inspired by the group's vision rather than a personal vision:

> As a result of my experience, I came to the conclusion that everyday Indians and poor people have a lot to contribute. I wanted to try to get people to be involved in articulating their own visions. I see a lot of beauty and intelligence and sharing in our communities. I would like to build on that. (Mankiller, 1992)

Leaders like Mankiller, who practice invisible leadership, look to the true heart of the community and know that the leadership must pass on to others. "I try to make decisions that are in the interest of the Cherokee Nation after listening to a lot of people and getting input from all kinds of folks," she said. It's about their collective vision, not about her own. "I really see myself as a temporary person; I'm here for a while, and then I pass the leadership on, and somebody else continues." Mankiller, who died in 2010, left a legacy of powerful invisible leadership. She was far from invisible personally, yet she kept her focus on the tribe's core purpose and legacy.

Illustrations From Business

Colors restaurant in New York is Manhattan's first cooperatively owned restaurant. It is run by former workers from the legendary Windows on the World restaurant (in Tower One of the World Trade Center). It is a self-governing organization, founded on the idea that everyone who works there has to be an owner. Their inspiring purpose came from their desire to move forward as a tribute to the 73 workers who died at the restaurant on 9/11 (Casimir, 2006). Restaurant worker–owners decided to share their diverse cultures as American immigrants through food from their countries of origin. The staff of owners includes 44 immigrants from 22 countries. They operate under the premise that everyone has to have the same share—an equal say in the restaurant. Its purpose not only inspires and organizes the business but also attracts customers, who come for the good food as well as to support the worker–owners' purpose of honoring their lost colleagues, as can be seen in recent Yelp restaurant review postings.

Béla Hatvany is an iconic pioneer in the information industry and was cofounder in 1983 of SilverPlatter, one of the first companies to produce commercial reference databases on CD-ROMs for libraries and other users. Companies he founded have been responsible for the first online public access catalog (OPAC), the first CD-ROMs, the first networked CD-ROM, the first client-server library databases, and some of the earliest Internet library database retrieval engines (Baczewski, 1994).

Since he sold SilverPlatter in 2001 for a purported $113 million, Hatvany has had the resources to dedicate himself to buying and working with purpose-oriented businesses around the world, including Classical.com,

JustGiving, Credo Reference, Productorial, Mustardseed Charitable Trust, and Coreweb. In turn, these companies have helped him to develop a business philosophy that empowers others and produces companies that are strikingly successful by any measure.

One of Hatvany's approaches is to sit with members of one of his enterprises, and listen. This may be just one or two days a year, since he does not manage his companies. "This is leadership not management. It is not directing or managing outcomes. It is inquiring deeply and thus drawing forth the joint understandings hidden in the spaces between all of the knowledge of the participants in the inquiry," he told us (Hatvany, 2012).

A bedrock criterion for his work is "to serve all constituents in a balanced way" (Hatvany, 2000). He defines constituents as the "customers, our business partners, our employees and our investors—all must be served in a balanced way" (Hatvany, 2000).

To do so, he believes that leaders have a role in holding shared values, because behind a powerful purpose are compelling and commonly held values:

> Organizations don't have values, people do, so it is up to the leader to be the persistent carrier of these values . . . reminding everyone in the organization of how they guide actions. For me these values must always be centered on the imperative of serving everyone in a balanced way. (Hatvany, 2012)

His thinking has evolved to where he sees all of the world as what he terms *corpus humanitatis,* a great human "corporation" or "body" connected by the Internet, an ecology of limitless possibilities. In his own words,

> I wish to enable an "ecology" in which all experience themselves to be well-served. I experience a world whose abundance is made available by human collaboration. . . . Money [commerce] is made of human agreement and enables this collaboration on a world-wide scale. (Hatvany, 2012)

Recently, leadership scholar James MacGregor Burns met with Hatvany to discuss leadership, and Burns remarked that Hatvany embodied and made real in a practical way his ideas about transforming leadership (personal communication, October 9, 2010).

Illustration From Social Movements

The work of the Women's Political Council (WPC) provides an example of invisible leadership committed to achieving an inspirational goal. Prior to the Montgomery, Alabama, bus boycott, a group of black women activists, who were members of the WPC, began the fight against segregation in their city by targeting Montgomery's segregated bus-seating practices. Jo Ann Robinson played a key role in initiating the WPC-orchestrated boycott. David Garrow's description of Robinson captures the essence of invisible leadership in action:

> Mrs. Robinson remains generally hesitant to claim for herself the historical credit that she deserves for launching the Montgomery Bus Boycott of 1955–1956. Although her story fully and accurately describes how it was she, during the night and early morning hours of December 1 and 2, 1955, who actually started the boycott on its way, it is only with some gentle encouragement that she will acknowledge herself as "the instigator of the movement to start the boycott." Even then, however, she seeks to emphasize that no special credit ought to go to herself or to any other single individual. Very simply, she says, "the black women did it." (Robinson, 1987, p. xv)

What Invisible Leadership Is Not

When people first hear the term *invisible leadership,* they often assume it means something different from the concept as we define it. We mean the common purpose is the invisible leader that inspires leaders and followers to take action on its behalf. We would like to clarify what our concept of invisible leadership is not.

It is not leadership that no one recognizes or acknowledges. Leaders and members of the organization know and value the work that others do to advance the purpose (like Jo Ann Robinson or Brian Lamb), even though much of their leadership may be internal to the organization, behind-the-scenes, quiet, unassuming, or not visible to those outside the organization.

Invisible leadership is not rendering individuals invisible. Certain groups of people in society, such as women, minorities, older people, or people with disabilities, are often made to feel invisible in their organizations. This is an important area of inquiry, which we have written about in earlier work but do not pursue here, and it is not what we mean by invisible leadership.

Invisible leadership does not mean that leaders or followers are invisible. Like Wilma Mankiller, people who use invisible leadership can be highly visible, or they can be deliberately in the background, like Jo Ann Robinson or Brian Lamb. They may choose either foreground or background leadership, and some are thrust into visibility as embodiments and advocates of their group's common purpose.

Invisible leadership is not a leadership substitute. On the contrary, there is plenty of leadership taking place by positional and nonpositional leaders at all levels of the organization. Positional leaders who engage in invisible leadership may have different functions from the leader roles in classic theories, because many organizational members are able to take action or lead based on a clear understanding of and commitment to the purpose. There are, however, essential functions for positional leaders, founders, and informal leaders. Béla Hatvany plays an essential role in the companies he is part of, as did Wilma Mankiller, Brian Lamb, and Jo Ann Robinson. All of them have personal traits of humility, emotional intelligence, and powers of listening and inquiry. But each of them understands deeply that the organization's success depends not on single leaders as much as the purpose, the group's shared work, and the relationships formed in "the space between." When leaders and members join in the invisible leadership of the organization, amazing things are possible.

Overview of the Book

The remaining chapters provide insight into the concept of invisible leadership through insights from different cultures, theories, our original research, and experiences of organizational members. Chapter 2 describes ancient and modern ideas that contribute to the foundation of invisible leadership. It includes concepts from Chinese, African, and Native American traditions together with modern theories of transforming leadership, servant leadership, convergence theory, and shared leadership concepts. In Chapter 3, we explore the ethics of invisible leadership by examining the moral implications of various types of common purpose and the group actions that ensue from implementing each type. Chapter 4 provides the results of our survey research, which examines the indicators of invisible leadership in 21 award-winning North American and international companies and non-profit organizations. Chapter 5 uses the extensive comments provided by survey respondents to understand their personal experiences with invisible leadership in these organizations. Finally, Chapter 6 focuses on advice and possibilities for the practice of invisible leadership and implications for future research.

References

Accenture. (2006). *Leadership in customer service: Building the trust.* Retrieved March 9, 2012, from http://www.accenture.com/us-en/Pages/insight-public-leadership-customer-service-building-trust-summary.aspx

Baczewski, P. (1994). *The Internet unleashed: Volume 1.* Retrieved August 22, 2012, from http://en.wikipedia.org/wiki/Béla_Hatvany#cite_note-2

Barton, E. F., III, & Sullivan, H. S. (1996). *Harry Stack Sullivan* (Makers of Modern Psychotherapy series). London, UK: Routledge.

Casimir, L. (2006, January 6). New window on taste. Colors eatery rises from WTC. *New York Daily News,* p. 21.

Farhi, P. (2012, March 19). For C-SPAN founder, a quiet exit. *The Washington Post,* p. C01.

Follett, M. P. (1949/1987). *Freedom & co-ordination: Lectures in business organization.* New York, NY: Garland.

Frantzich, S., & Sullivan, J. (1996). *The C-SPAN revolution.* Norman: University of Oklahoma Press.

Hatvany, B. (2000, February). Miles Conrad Memorial Lecture. Retrieved August 22, 2012, from http://www.nfais.org/page/46-Béla-hatvany-2000

Hatvany, B. (2012, August 20). Interview with Georgia Sorenson.

Hazlett, T. W. (1996). *Changing channels: C-SPAN's Brian Lamb on how unfiltered reporting and media competition are transforming American politics.* Retrieved January 2, 2003, from http://www.reason.com/9603/fe.LAMB.text.html

Kelley, R. E. (1988). In praise of followers. *Harvard Business Review, 66*(6), 142–148.

Kelley, R. E. (1992). *The power of followership: How to create leaders people want to follow . . . and followers who lead themselves.* New York, NY: Doubleday.

Lamb, B. (1999, November 20). Interview with G. J. Sorenson.

Light, P. C. (2001). *To restore and renew: Now is the time to rebuild the federal public service.* Brookings Institution. Retrieved October 14, 2007, from http://www.brookings.edu/articles/2001/11governance_light.aspx

Mankiller, W. (1992). Interview with G. J. Sorenson.

NASA. (n.d.) *Dark matter: Introduction.* Retrieved February 23, 2012, from http://imagine.gsfc.nasa.gov/docs/science/know_11/dark_matter.html

Pleasants, A. K. (2001). Trust and intimacy: Eudora Welty, who died July 23, captured the south in pictures as well as words. *Smithsonian, 32*(7), 38.

Robinson, J. G. (1987). *The Montgomery bus boycott and the women who started it: The memoir of Jo Ann Gibson Robinson.* Knoxville: The University of Tennessee Press.

Seifter, H. (2009). Interview with G. R. Hickman and G. J. Sorenson.

Seifter, H., & Economy, P. (2001). *Leadership ensemble: Lessons in collaborative management from the world's only conductorless orchestra.* New York, NY: Times Books.

Sorenson, G., & Hickman, G. R. (2002). Invisible leadership: Acting on behalf of a common purpose. In C. Cherrey & L. R. Matusak (Eds.), *Building leadership bridges* (pp. 7–24). College Park, MD: James MacGregor Burns Academy of Leadership.

2

Illuminating the Secrets of Ancient, Hidden, and Modern Wisdom

Ancient and Hidden Wisdom

The idea of a common purpose inspiring people to initiate leadership is not a new concept; in fact, it is a very old one. Invisible leadership has deep roots in ancient societies, especially in Chinese, African, and Native American cultures.

In the Chinese tradition, the Taijitu symbol above is familiar to many, representing the one (the individual) in many (the group). The symbol, referred to as yin and yang in the West, does not represent opposing forces but rather interpenetrating and complementary opposites that are one and many, male and female, dark and light.

Individuals and roles (such as the role of leader) are not separate from the group, and there is no traditional Chinese word for *leader* as Westerners understand it. Invisibility and visibility are both equal and significant.

The Chinese classic *I Ching* (Book of Changes) refers to invisible leadership as *chi zoshiki* (chi invisibility), to which the philosophers accord great status. Taoist leadership is invisible and is the highest and most effective leadership according to the tenets of its belief system. It is natural, unassuming, open, all-embracing, down-to-earth, selfless, calm, considerate, courteous, inconspicuous, defenseless, centered, grounded, aware (of what is happening and how things happen), flexible, flowing, fluid, soft, and yielding. It involves consciousness of unity, integrity, compassion, frugality, and modesty. Since the group and the individual are one, Taoist leaders interact and facilitate the collective work of invisible leadership by gently supporting people to lead themselves. This enables group agency and strong shared bonds among participants that move them to say, "We did it ourselves" (Heider, 1985, p. 33).

This brings us to the conundrum at the heart of the matter: Is invisible leadership about individuals or is it a groupwide phenomenon? Or both? Or perhaps it is a Gordian knot, as psychologist Margaret Rioch said, "When I look for the group I see myself, when I look for myself, I see the group" (Rioch, 1971). We assert that invisible leadership is a groupwide phenomenon. It is inspired and sustained by the common purpose and carried out through shared leadership by individuals who willingly perform leader or follower roles.

There may be a Taoist master, a Wilma Mankiller, Jo Ann Robinson, Béla Hatvany, or Brian Lamb involved in the group, or there may not be. Or one could argue that these individuals are *a product of the group rather than the producer of the group.*

Centuries of Western thought have assumed that leadership is an ability or capacity of an individual to influence others. It is individually based or conferred. Social psychologist Geert Hofstede's (1980, 2001) groundbreaking cross-cultural work on the influence of culture ranked the United States as highest on individualism, and nowhere is this more apparent than in our modern views of leadership.

Recently, however, research has demonstrated the utility of viewing leadership as a groupwide phenomenon, which is what author W. Drath contends is a "communal capacity and a communal achievement" (as quoted in Dent, Higgens, & Wharf, 2005, p. 646). The Chinese are ranked "a highly collectivist culture" on Hofstede's scale for "communal," quite the opposite of the United States. A shared bond is essential to a way of life in China and aligns with our core observation in Chapter 1 that there is a strong shared bond among participants pursuing a common purpose.

As we found in our work at the Chinese Leadership Academy at Pudong and the People's Republic of Public Administration, the Chinese conception

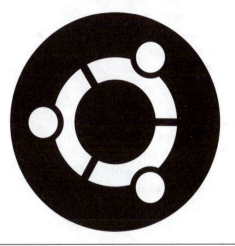

Note: Ubuntu® is a trademark of Canonical Ltd. and is used under license from Canonical Ltd. Points of view or opinions in this publication do not necessarily represent the views, opinions, policies, or positions of Canonical Ltd. or imply any affiliation with Ubuntu or the Ubuntu project.

of leadership is now influenced by the West, but there are still strong undertones of Taoist and Confucian leadership just beneath the surface.

The traditional African concept of *ubuntu* contributes to the notion of action on behalf of the common purpose. The philosophy of ubuntu leadership comes from the traditional African view of leadership and life as a collective function. Ubuntu means "a person can only be a person through others" (Mikgoro, 1998). It exists only in the interaction between people and focuses on shared humanity and collective unity to promote the good of the community. Ubuntu embodies the belief that an individual's most effective behavior occurs when he or she is working toward the common good of the group. It exemplifies our core observation from Chapter 1: the presence of a compelling and deeply held common purpose. The ubuntu symbol above shows a group around a table, with all figures equal and engaged. Accordingly, individual self-interest or self-centeredness does not advance the common purpose. In postapartheid South Africa, the concept is being restored and infused into education, law, and workplace practices, including the common greeting on the street of "I see you" rather than "How are you?"

Invisible leadership in the Native American sense engages the group in a "vision quest" centered on the purpose for which the group was given life (Reyes & Perreault, 1993). The principles of leadership in many Native American communities are group-based—council and wholeness. Basic to the concept of council are the values of respect, empathy, and trust, which are vital to developing the ability to see through another's eyes or "walk in another person's moccasins." Wholeness focuses on balance, connectedness, authenticity, and a harmonious relationship with the powers of the universe. Again, it manifests as a whole rather than a part. Individuals in groups are viewed as water carriers (symbolized above) and as the "person who does what needs to be done when it needs to be done" (Bryant, 1996) without respect to credit, position, or role.

Like one of our core observations about invisible leadership, in many Native American cultures there is a readiness to use individual strengths in either leader or follower roles with or without visible recognition or personal ego. The council process, which is distinct from the tribal political structure, is first and foremost intended to move leadership and followership toward community (Reyes & Perrault, 1993), and the perspective includes ancestors, present members, and future generations.

These concepts from Chinese, African, and Native American traditions provide a foundation from ancient wisdom for collective leadership of the common purpose. Participants in our study described the closeness of their bonds to each other, developed through a consciousness of unity and their quest for a purpose greater than each member.

Modern Wisdom: Building on Existing Theories

Several contemporary theories have helped to lay the groundwork for the concept of invisible leadership. Invisible leadership is a complementary but necessary addition to the panoply of ideas. Some of these ideas include Follett's (1949/1987) concept of invisible leadership, transforming leadership, transformational leadership, servant leadership, convergence theory and collective processes, and shared leadership. The concept of invisible leadership does not replace these current theories. Instead, it benefits from them and brings to the forefront a form of leadership that has been understated or unrecognized. Figure 2.1 shows existing theories that have provided the building blocks for invisible leadership.

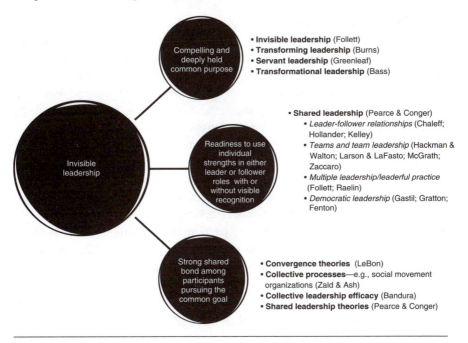

Figure 2.1   Theories that contribute to invisible leadership

Early Concept of Invisible Leadership

Mary Parker Follett conceived that leaders and followers are both follow-ing the invisible leader, which is the common purpose. Leadership, according to Follett, depends on depth of conviction to the purpose, the power that comes from this conviction, the ability to share this conviction with others, and the ability to articulate the purpose. She proposes that loyalty to the com-mon purpose (the invisible leader) connects leaders and followers together in "the strongest possible bond of union" (Follett, 1949/1987, p. 55).

Transforming Leadership and the Common Purpose

Our colleague, political scientist James MacGregor Burns (1978), focuses on the common purpose in his theory of transforming leadership. He asserts that

> leadership is nothing if not linked to collective purpose; that the effectiveness of leaders must be judged not by their press clippings but by actual social change measured by intent and by the satisfaction of human needs and expec-tations. (p. 3) . . . Whatever the separate interests persons might hold, they are presently or potentially united in the pursuit of "higher" goals, the realization of which is tested by the achievement of significant change that represents the collective or pooled interest of leaders and followers. (pp. 425–426)

He describes the leadership process as "leaders inducing followers to act for certain goals" (Burns, 1978, p. 19) that represent the collective values and motivations of leaders and followers. The central focus of Burns's theory is on raising the level of motivation and morality of the people in the process. He says "transforming leadership ultimately becomes moral in that it raises the level of human conduct and ethical aspirations of both the leader and the led, and thus it has a transforming effect on both" (p. 20). Thus, leadership is not something that is done "to" or "for" the group, but something that is done together collectively.

Transforming leadership, however, assumes that leaders must first persuade followers to act. This is indeed a viable and effective form of leadership, but it is different from our concept of invisible leadership. By contrast, invisible leadership involves participants coming together because of their belief and commitment to the common purpose with little or no inducement from leaders. Their shared experiences or dedication to the cause attract them to follow the invisible leader by serving in visible and unseen roles as leaders or participants, much like the "water carriers" in some Native American cultures we noted previously. Jo Ann Robinson's group, the Women's Political Council, circulated notices to the African American community about the Montgomery, Alabama, bus boycott, and many ministers found out on the Sunday prior to the boycott that their congregations planned to support it, "with or without their ministers' leadership" (Robinson, 1987, p. 53). The ministers found, to their surprise, "it was time for them to catch up with the masses" (p. 53). Once the ministers realized the one-day boycott was successful, they met with and selected Martin Luther King Jr. as the public face and visible leader of the movement. Contemporary causes and movements, such as the environmental movement, the LGBT movement, and the animal rights movement, often attract participants based on the charisma of purpose, not solely because of charismatic or persuasive leaders.

Servant Leadership

Robert Greenleaf's (1977) concept of servant leadership focuses on the common purpose, using the term *goal* to mean overarching purpose. Like Burns, Greenleaf contends it is the "leader" in this process who shows the way, induces others to follow, provides structure, and models risk-taking behavior in servant leadership. Greenleaf proposes that both individuals and institutions can act as leaders for the purpose of serving each other to build a good society. Even when institutions, through their trustees, are servant leaders, the institution—not the common purpose—ultimately exerts the strongest influence.

Mutuality of purpose among leaders and followers is an important factor in transforming and servant leadership, but the deep organizing purpose does not occupy the central motivating function in these concepts. Furthermore, invisible leadership broadens the spectrum of leadership beyond the seminal influence of a single leader or group of trustees to include the many individuals, seen and unseen, inside and outside of the organization or group, who willingly take on roles as leaders or followers based on the powerful appeal of a common purpose.

Transformational Leadership and Inspirational Motivation

Psychologists Bernard Bass and Bruce Avolio's research on transformational leadership identifies a form of leadership that motivates others to do more than they originally intended or thought possible (Bass & Riggio, 2006). Similar to the common purpose in invisible leadership, they found that inspirational motivation is a significant contributor to high levels of performance by participants. Inspirational motivation occurs when "leaders involve followers in envisioning an attractive future state or compelling vision; they provide meaningful, challenging work and communicate clear expectations that encourage followers' commitment to the shared vision and goals" (Bass & Riggio, 2006, p. 6). Three other components contribute to Bass and Avolio's theory of transformational leadership: idealized influence (the leader serves as role model of high standards and ethical behavior), intellectual stimulation (the leader stimulates followers' innovation and creativity), and individualized consideration (the leader develops individual mentoring and coaching relationships with followers).

The source of inspiration and action is different in transformational leadership than it is in invisible leadership. Transformational leadership focuses on the characteristics and behaviors of a leader as the source of inspiration for followers to achieve exceptional outcomes, while invisible leadership focuses on the power of a compelling and deeply held common purpose to inspire leaders and followers to accomplish great results jointly.

Convergence Theory and Collective Processes

Certain group theories help to explain collective elements of invisible leadership, especially in social movement and nonprofit contexts. Convergence theory contends that people in collective processes join groups because they possess certain characteristics (Forsyth, 2010, p. 516). Forsyth explains that these groups are not unrelated collections of dissimilar people, but "the convergence of people with compatible needs, desires, motivations, and emotions" who join together to satisfy their needs (p. 516).

He cites further studies that shed light on why people engage in social activism through social movement organizations (McAdam, McCarthy, & Zald; Snow & Oliver, and Zald & Ash as cited in Forsyth, 2010, p. 516). These individuals have a sense of injustice, efficacy, and social identity (van Zomeren, Postmes, & Spears as cited in Forsyth, 2010, p. 516). They have a strong sense of fairness and an abhorrence of unjust treatment of themselves and others. At the same time, researchers found that individuals who join social movements are higher in personal efficacy or self-agency and believe that their actions can make a difference in the outcome (Snow & Oliver as cited in Forsyth, 2010, p. 516).

Another researcher discovered that "self-confidence, achievement orientation, need for autonomy, dominance, self-acceptance, and maturity are positively correlated with social activism" (Werner as cited in Forsyth, 2010, p. 516). Research also revealed that people who strongly identify with a group and its purpose (social identity) put more effort into reaching its goals (Klandermans as cited in Forsyth, 2010, p. 517). Like the concept of ubuntu, these social activists see their identity as intertwined with the group's identity and, as a result, view injustices or deprivation of the group even more negatively than injustices to themselves.

Shared Leadership

Shared leadership is "a dynamic, interactive influence process among individuals in groups in which the objective is to lead one another to the achievement of group or organizational goals or both" (Pearce & Conger, 2003, p. 1). Leadership is broadly distributed among participants, unlike traditional top-down leadership processes, and entails lateral, upward, or downward influence on leaders and participants. Invisible leadership builds on several shared leadership concepts—leader-follower relations, teams and team leadership, and democratic leadership.

Leader-Follower Relations

In the last two decades or so, largely as a result of the work of social scientists Edwin Hollander (1978, 1997, 2009) and Robert Kelley (1988, 1992), students of leadership have acknowledged the interaction of leaders and participants—and their equal, but different, roles—as the process that energizes and propels leadership. Hollander (1978) was one of the early scholars who called attention to the essential and underrecognized contributions that followers make to leadership. He stressed that the process of leadership is not confined to a single leader but depends on other participants; yet it is easier for people outside the process to attribute leadership activities and outcomes to the leader, because his or her actions generally command more attention (p. 2) and accountability.

Organizational behaviorist Robert Kelley (1988) argues that leader and follower are flexible "roles" that participants assume to accomplish the group's ends. Their work is interdependent—both leaders and followers take part in leadership. Kelley explains that leadership and followership are equal but different roles sometimes played by the same people at different times. Leaders and followers participate as coleaders engaged in a process of "multiple leadership," in the words of Follett (1982). Individuals who assume leadership roles have the desire and willingness to lead as well as a clear vision and capabilities in interpersonal relations, communications, and organization (Kelley, 1988, p. 147).

Exemplary followers form the other equally important component of the equation and are distinguished by their capacity for self-management, strong commitment, and courage. Kelley (1992) indicates that leadership accounts for about 20% of the success in organizations, while followership is the real people factor that contributes about 80% toward a success (pp. 7–8). Followers bring forth the courage, tenacity, and endurance to stay the course in hard times and ultimately to achieve the common purpose. Kelley explains that some people volunteer or are solicited by the group to remain in certain long-term roles based on their willingness and capacity to serve; this service is similar to invisible leadership.

The idea of leader and follower/participant as "roles" is a significant concept for invisible leadership. Both roles are essential to pursuing and achieving the common purpose; neither leaders nor followers are expendable in the process. These roles are much more fluid in reality than leader-centric theories portray. (Leader-centric theories are those that focus on one positional leader in formal organizations, or one leader in informal ones.) The driving force of invisible leadership is the willingness of all participants to contribute their knowledge, expertise, and capabilities without regard to positional assignments or roles.

Management author Ira Chaleff's (2009) model of the courageous follower incorporates many of the concepts of exemplary followers but focuses more extensively on the element of courage in followership. His model identifies several dimensions of courage among followers: the courage to assume responsibility, the courage to serve, the courage to challenge, the courage to participate in transformation, the courage to take moral action, the courage to speak to the hierarchy, and the leader's courage to listen to followers (Chaleff, 2009, pp. 6–8). Many of these dimensions relate directly to the follower's responsibility to and ownership of the common purpose. For example, when describing the courage of followers to assume responsibility, Chaleff says, "The 'authority' to initiate comes from the courageous follower's understanding and ownership of the common purpose, and from the needs of those the organization serves" (p. 6). He contends that followers are as passionate as leaders in pursuing the common purpose and that followers should "value organizational harmony and their relationship with the leader, but not at the expense of the common purpose and their integrity" (Chaleff, 2009, p. 7).

Teams and Team Leadership

Leadership scholars and practitioners recognize the added value that teams bring to achieving organizational goals. Organizational communication scholar Susan Hill (2010) credits researchers such as Hackman and Walton, Larson and LaFasto, Zaccaro, and McGrath with developing concepts on teams and team leadership (pp. 241–243). Teams are organizational groups composed of members who are interdependent, who share common goals, and who must coordinate their activities to accomplish these goals (Hill, 2010, p. 241). Teams bring enhanced capacity and diverse contributions, beyond individual efforts, to the focused work of an organizational entity. Often, leadership in teams is dispersed even when there is a designated team leader. Self-directed (distributed leadership) and virtual teams (geographically dispersed participants, supported by information technology) contribute to the concept of invisible leadership through their emphasis on collaborative work and fluid leader–participant roles that focus on achieving the common purpose.

Multiple Leadership/Leaderful Practice

In 1928, Mary Parker Follett proposed the concept of "multiple leadership," which she described as widely diffused leadership (Follett, 1982, p. 253). Her observations of certain exceptional business leaders led her to remark that "leadership is creating a partnership in a common task, a joint responsibility" (p. 255).

Indeed, Follett was ahead of her time. Only in recent times have organizations begun to embrace multiple leadership. Business professor Joseph Raelin (2005) describes this concept in 21st century organizations as "leaderful practice," where everyone shares leadership (p. 18). Leaderful practice juxtaposes the traditional Western leadership model—leadership is serial, individual, controlling, and dispassionate—with an alternative approach—leadership is concurrent, collective, collaborative, and compassionate (p. 22).

Raelin's first tenet, leadership is concurrent, means that more than one leader can share power and operate at the same time to achieve the goals of an organization or community.

His second tenet, leadership is collective, denotes that leadership can be a plural function that facilitates people working together as leaders for the common purpose. He emphasizes that even when one person initiates an action, others can become involved and share leadership with the initiator.

The third tenet, leadership is collaborative, indicates that individual members may speak on behalf of the whole community. Participants in the process believe all members are equally valuable and their contributions and ideas deserve consideration. Members speak on behalf of the community with a focus on the common good and the views and feelings of other participants in mind.

The last tenet, leadership is compassionate, means "one extends unadulterated commitment to preserving the dignity of others" (Raelin, 2005, p. 23). Decisions for the whole community include consideration of the views of the stakeholders.

Democratic Leadership

Invisible leadership often encompasses democratic leadership processes and structures to attain the common purpose. Communications professor John Gastil (1994) defines democratic leadership as performing three functions: distributing responsibility among the membership, empowering group members, and aiding the group's decision-making process (p. 953). He indicates that most members of the group perform these functions and exchange leader and follower roles often. Functions of democratic leadership seem particularly appropriate for invisible leadership where participants come into the process willingly due to their attraction and commitment to the common purpose.

Traci Fenton, CEO of WorldBlu, whose company publishes an annual list of Most Democratic Workplaces, comments that democratic leadership does not suggest that leaders surrender control. "It simply means that a company is committed to a system that empowers people—rather than just the CEO—to generate solutions and make decisions" (Fenton, 2008, p. 9). Large, small, and medium-sized organizations have the capacity to implement democratic leadership practices and tailor them to their culture, context, and participants. The Orpheus Chamber Orchestra mentioned in Chapter 1 is an example of a small nonprofit organization that embraces democratic leadership. Fenton also cites the example of DaVita, an independent dialysis services company with more than 30,000 employees, that turned around its struggling business through democratic practices. The CEO and his team initiated decentralization of 1,300 clinics, democratic decision making and voting on a range of issues, and Town Hall meetings for sharing information as well as Voice of the Village meetings for team members to ask questions of the senior leadership (Fenton, 2008, p. 9). The company's profitability and stock value skyrocketed.

While democratic structures and practices differ in each organization, business professor Lynda Gratton (2004) offers six tenets that form the basis of any democratic enterprise. These are as follows:

1. The relationship between the organization and the individual is adult-to-adult.

2. Individuals are seen primarily as investors actively building and deploying their human capital.

3. Individuals are able to develop their natures and express their diverse qualities.

4. Individuals are able to participate in determining the conditions of their association.

5. The liberty of some individuals is not at the expense of others.

6. Individuals have accountabilities and obligations both to themselves and the organization. (p. 35)

Invisible leadership often embodies democratic leadership and structure, but these factors alone are not sufficient to compose invisible leadership.

Collective Leadership Efficacy

At the heart of shared leadership processes is collective leadership efficacy. Psychologist Albert Bandura developed the concept of collective efficacy, defined as

> a collective sense that members have that, together, they can perform a par-
> ticular task. This definition emphasizes that collective efficacy is a property
> of the group; it represents a belief of collective competence (or incompetence)
> that is strongly shared among all group members to the point that it becomes
> a defining characteristic of the group as a whole. (Zaccaro & Cracraft, 2004,
> p. 412)

A group's perceived collective efficacy is not simply the sum of individual efficacy beliefs; it is a property that emerges from the group (Bandura, 2000, p. 76). Findings from research on collective efficacy indicate that perceptions of high collective efficacy by a group help its members sustain motivation to achieve its common purpose, facilitate stronger staying power in the face of difficulties, and contribute to high performance accomplishments by the group (Bandura, 2000, p. 78). Again, these factors are present but not sufficient for invisible leadership.

Traditional leadership models ascribe responsibility to the leader for focusing attention on the purpose and generating collective efficacy among group members. In shared leadership settings, interdependent groups, communities, or organizations can foster collective leadership efficacy through their mutual efforts, including commitment to the common purpose.

The ancient, hidden, and modern forms of wisdom touched upon in this chapter illuminate seminal concepts that invisible leadership draws upon and yet distinguishes itself from, too. Other processes and practices such as organizational commitment—commitment to the organization's mission by all members (Yukl, 2012); engagement—participation or performance in an organization that is above the norm and aligned with the organization's interest (Gratton, 2004); job satisfaction—participants' feelings or attitudes about the job itself, pay, opportunities, coworkers, and so on (Hughes, Ginnett, & Curphy, 2009); and vision—"a realistic, credible, attractive future for the organization" (Nanus, 1992, p. 7) are also brought together in the development and nurturing of invisible leadership.

In the next chapter, we will explore the moral implications of various types of common purpose and group actions with the hope of guiding organizations toward the ethical use of invisible leadership.

References

Bandura, A. (2000). Exercise of human agency through collective efficacy. *Current Directions in Psychological Science, 9*(3), 75–78.

Bass, B. M., & Riggio, R. E. (2006). *Transformational leadership*. Mahwah, NJ: Lawrence Erlbaum.

Bryant, M. (1996, October). *Contrasting American and Native American views of leadership*. Paper presented at the Annual Meeting of the University Council for Educational Administration, Louisville, KY.

Burns, J. M. (1978). *Leadership*. New York, NY: Harper Torchbooks.

Chaleff, I. (2009). *The courageous follower: Standing up to & for our leaders*. San Francisco, CA: Berrett-Koehler.

Dent, E., Higgens, M. E., & Wharf, D. (2005). Spirituality and leadership: An empirical review of definitions, distinctions, and embedded assumptions. *The Leadership Quarterly, 5,* 646.

Fenton, T. (2008, May 6). Even big companies are embracing a democratic style. *The Christian Science Monitor, 100,* p. 9.

Follett, M. P. (1949/1987). *Freedom & co-ordination: Lectures in business organization*. New York, NY: Garland.

Follett, M. P. (1982). *Dynamics of administration: The collected papers of Mary Parker Follett* (E. Fox & L. F. Urwick, Eds.). New York, NY: Hippocrene Books.

Forsyth, D. R. (2010). *Group dynamics.* Belmont, CA: Wadsworth, Cengage Learning.

Gastil, J. (1994). A definition and illustration of democratic leadership. *Human Relations, 47*(8), 953–975. Retrieved June 28, 2010, from ABI/INFORM Global (Document ID: 49069).

Gratton, L. (2004). *The democratic enterprise: Liberating your business with freedom, flexibility and commitment.* London, UK: FT Prentice Hall.

Greenleaf, R. K. (1977). *Servant leadership: A journey into the nature of legitimate power and greatness.* New York, NY: Paulist Press.

Heider, J. (1985). *The tao of leadership: Lao Tzu's Tao Te Ching adapted for a new age.* New York, NY: Bantam Books.

Hill, S. E. K. (2010). Team leadership. In P. G. Northouse (Ed.), *Leadership: Theory and practice* (5th ed., pp. 241–270). Thousand Oaks, CA: Sage.

Hofstede, G. (1980). *Culture's consequences: International differences in work-related values.* Beverly Hills, CA: Sage.

Hofstede, G. (2001). *Culture's consequences: Comparing values, behaviors, institutions, and organizations across nations.* Thousand Oaks, CA: Sage.

Hollander, E. P. (1978). *Leadership dynamics: A practical guide to effective relationships.* New York, NY: Free Press.

Hollander, E. P. (1997). How and why active followers matter in leadership. In E. P. Hollander & L. R. Offermann (Eds.), *The balance of leadership and followership* (pp. 11–28). College Park, MD: James MacGregor Burns Academy of Leadership, University of Maryland, Kellogg Leadership Studies Project.

Hollander, E. P. (2009). *Inclusive leadership: The essential leader–follower relationship.* New York, NY: Routledge.

Hughes, R. L., Ginnett, R. C., & Curphy, G. J. (2009). *Leadership: Enhancing the lessons of experience.* New York, NY: McGraw-Hill/Irwin.

Kelley, R. E. (1988). In praise of followers. *Harvard Business Review, 66*(6), 142–148.

Kelley, R. E. (1992). *The power of followership: How to create leaders people want to follow . . . and followers who lead themselves.* New York, NY: Doubleday.

Mikgoro, J. Y. (1998). *Ubuntu and the law in South Africa.* Retrieved October 14, 2007, from http://www.puk.ac.za/lawper/1998–1/mokgoro-ubuntu.html

Nanus, B. (1992). *Visionary leadership.* San Francisco CA: Jossey-Bass.

Pearce, C. L., & Conger, J. A. (Eds.). (2003). *Shared leadership: Reframing the hows and whys of leadership.* Thousand Oaks, CA: Sage.

Peters, T. J., and Video Publishing House (Directors). (1988). *The leadership alliance* [Video/DVD]. Des Plaines, IL: Video Publishing House.

Raelin, J. A. (2005). We the leaders: In order to form a leaderful organization. *Journal of Leadership & Organizational Studies, 12*(2), 18–30.

Reyes, R., & Perreault, J. (1993). Wholeness and council: A Native American perspective on leadership. *Proteus: A Journal of Ideas, 10*(1), 43–46.

Rioch, M. J. (1971). "All we like sheep" (Isaiah 53:6): Followers and leaders. *Psychiatry, 34*, 258–273.

Robinson, J. G. (1987). *The Montgomery bus boycott and the women who started it: The memoir of Jo Ann Gibson Robinson.* Knoxville: The University of Tennessee Press.

Yukl, G. (2012). *Leadership in organizations.* Upper Saddle River, NJ: Pearson Education.

Zaccaro, S. J., & Cracraft, M. (2004). Efficacy. In G. R. Goethals, G. J. Sorenson, & J. M. Burns (Eds.), *Encyclopedia of leadership* (vol. 1, pp. 410–414). Thousand Oaks, CA: Sage Reference.

3

Exposing the Ethics
of Invisible Leadership

Scholars, practitioners, and students invariably ask us: Is there an underlying assumption in invisible leadership that the common purpose is always ethical? Can a group achieve an ethical common purpose using unethical means? Just because a group of people willingly engage in leadership based on a powerful purpose does not mean the purpose is inherently moral, or that the leadership to achieve that purpose is ethical. Groups have led both humanitarian and inhumane endeavors based on their dedication to a common purpose, and they have led efforts to achieve ethical results using unethical means.

We believe the common purpose, its leaders, and its participants should promote ethical means and ends in invisible leadership. Philosopher Al Gini (2004) uses the concepts of philosopher John Rawls to define the role of ethics in leadership and daily life:

> Minimally, "good behavior" intends no harm and respects the rights of all affected, and "bad behavior" is willfully or negligently trampling on the rights and interests of others. Ethics, then, tries to find a way to protect one person's individual rights and needs against and alongside the rights and needs of others. (p. 29)

According to leadership scholar and philosopher Terry Price (2004), to assess whether participants in the leadership process have led ethically requires assessment of "the rightness of their means, the goodness of their ends, and the virtue of their characters and intentions" (p. 463). We contend

---

Note: The authors would like to thank Terry Price for his comments and advice on this chapter.

the ethics of invisible leadership *should* encompass these moral features and fully promote the development and practice of ethical invisible leadership. Even so, there are purposes and actors that ostensibly fit the description of invisible leadership but vary in the extent to which they meet their moral responsibility to people within and outside the group.

As is indicated in Figure 3.1, the common purpose of an organizing group can range from ethical and helpful to unethical and harmful to people within and outside the group. The figure illustrates three prototypes of the common purpose, with examples of each organizing group, potential beneficiaries, and potential opponents or aggrieved groups. The common purpose in Prototype I entails promoting human and environmental well-being and doing no harm. An ethical purpose with such compelling power frequently involves generating environmental stewardship, working for the rights of disenfranchised groups or individuals, improving public services, or providing access to greater opportunities. Examples of groups doing this kind of work include various kinds of movements (including environmental, human rights, civil rights, gay rights, and women's rights) and many nonprofit or nongovernmental organizations (NGOs) as well as governmental or community service providers such as firefighters and EMTs.

Prototype II focuses on an ethical common purpose of a specific group or entity that organizes to serve its members and deliver products, services, or activities. This purpose may develop the capacity of group members, generate consumer products or services, establish or sustain religious values and practices, or produce a winning team. Examples of these groups include professional organizations, businesses, religious institutions, sports teams, and nonprofit institutions such as universities, among others. The common purpose is not typically harmful to its members or others outside the group.

Prototype III depicts an unethical common purpose that focuses on achieving the aim of a specific group or entity; but, in this case, the purpose is generally harmful to the well-being of target groups. The organizing group's intent is to deny rights and privileges to target groups, or to claim perceived entitlements or superiority that result in banning, excluding, restricting, or persecuting other groups. Examples of this prototype are extremists, terrorists, supremacist groups, and repressive regimes.

These three prototypes represent only a sample of the possible purposes, beneficiaries, and organizing groups that may exist. In reality, there are many variations and gradations of these prototypes. Some may connect, intersect, correspond, or conflict with others in a web of relationships between and among prototypes.

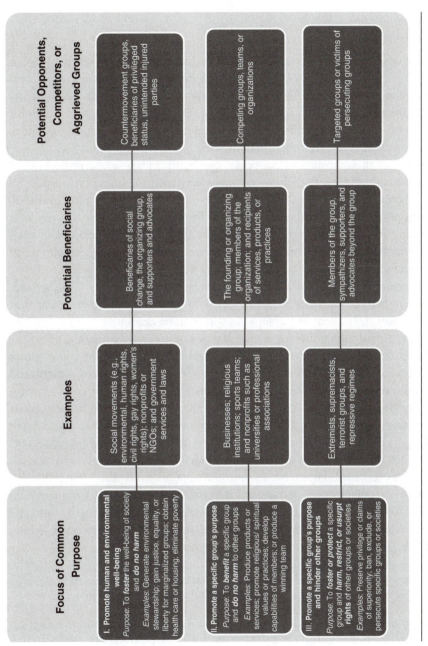

Figure 3.1 Ethical Implications of Invisible Leadership

Focus of Common Purpose

I. **Promote human and environmental well-being**
Purpose: To *foster* the well-being of society and *do no harm*
Examples: Generate environmental stewardship; gain justice, equality, or liberty for marginalized groups; obtain health care or housing; eliminate poverty

II. **Promote a specific group's purpose**
Purpose: To *benefit* a specific group and *do no harm* to other groups
Examples: Produce products or services; promote religious/ spiritual values or practices; develop capabilities of members; or produce a winning team

III. **Promote a specific group's purpose and hinder other groups**
Purpose: To *foster or protect* a specific group and *harm, restrict, or usurp rights* of other groups or societies
Examples: Preserve privilege or claims of superiority; ban, exclude, or persecute specific groups or societies

Examples

Social movements (e.g., environmental, human rights, civil rights, gay rights, women's rights); nonprofits or NGOs; and government services and laws

Businesses; religious institutions; sports teams; and nonprofits such as universities or professional associations

Extremists, supremacists, terrorist groups, and repressive regimes

Potential Beneficiaries

Beneficiaries of social change, the organizing group, and supporters and advocates

The founding or organizing group; members of the organization; and recipients of services, products, or practices

Members of the group, sympathizers, supporters, and advocates beyond the group

Potential Opponents, Competitors, or Aggrieved Groups

Countermovement groups, beneficiaries of privileged status, unintended injured parties

Competing groups, teams, or organizations

Targeted groups or victims of persecuting groups

Light, Shadowy, and Opposing
Sides of Invisible Leadership

The Light Side

The inspiration of an ethical common purpose is not limited to social movements or nonprofit organizations, as Figure 3.1 shows. Invisible leadership can be found in a business where members at all levels demonstrate exceptional commitment to create and sustain an inspiring common purpose, ensure equitable and respectful treatment of each other, and produce products or services that members of society want or need.

Many of these businesses adopt a triple bottom line—social responsibility, volunteerism, and profitability—that intersects with the common purpose of social action in Prototype I to produce benefits for the organization and society. Employees of the company Interface, for instance, manufacture modular carpeting and foster ecological sustainability through their products and environmentally conscious manufacturing processes (Interface, 2008). Employees of Timberland, producers of clothing and footwear, commit themselves to "civic engagement, environmental stewardship and global human rights" (Timberland, n.d.). Timberland provides its employees with 40 hours of paid leave per year to volunteer their talent and abilities in surrounding communities and up to six months of paid sabbaticals for service leaves in social justice organizations.

Organizations like Interface and Timberland follow the invisible leader by allowing their business–social purpose to lead their members' actions and chart the direction for their companies. More important, their company stories demonstrate that leaders and participants can discover or cultivate their charismatic purpose over time by being open to new opportunities and being willing to change or alter course. Chairman Ray Anderson of Interface says that when he was asked to spearhead an environmental task force and give the kickoff speech, he did not have an environmental mission other than following the law. By coincidence, he received a book, *The Ecology of Commerce* by Paul Hawken (1993), prior to preparing his speech. After reading the book, he experienced a "spear in the chest" moment, an epiphany (Anderson & White, 2009, p. 13). Anderson told the task force during his speech,

> We are going to shoulder our ecological responsibilities. . . . Every business has three big issues to face: what we take from the earth; what we make with all the energy and material; and what we waste along the way. We're going to push the envelope until we no longer take anything the earth can't easily renew. We're going to keep pushing until all our products are made from recycled or renewable materials. And we are not going to stop pushing until all our waste is biodegradable or recyclable, until nothing we make ends up as pollution. No gases up a smokestack, no dirty water out a pipe, no piles of carpet scraps to dump. Nothing. (p. 17)

Anderson, the members of his company, and many other colleagues in his industry took this mission to heart. In the Interface situation, it was the company chairs that launched a renewed purpose, but it is the purpose itself that draws people to the work. Today, scientists and engineers from the most prestigious universities are inspired by this "charisma of purpose" to come and work for Interface.

Timberland, like Interface, enhanced its purpose over time. When Jeffrey Swartz, now president and CEO, was first approached by the nonprofit community service organization City Year, it asked for a donation of boots for its corps members. After hearing more about City Year's mission, Swartz wanted to get Timberland's employees involved in the work. Many Timberland employees were already actively engaged in community service. Swartz created the Path of Service program to facilitate the company's volunteering efforts in City Year and many other nonprofit organizations. Timberland now fully integrates social justice tenets into its common purpose.

Some groups form around a common purpose that promotes the development or satisfaction of their members exclusively; these include support groups, many professional associations, and social or hobby groups; other groups serve their members and simultaneously produce outcomes that benefit the general public. The Orpheus Chamber Orchestra, mentioned in Chapter 1, formed to provide every musician in the group an opportunity to use his or her full talents and create extraordinary music using a democratic leadership process. In addition to developing their own talents and capabilities, they entertain appreciative audiences around the world through their public performances.

The Shadowy Side

The shadowy side of invisible leadership occurs when people are inspired by a common purpose that achieves their aims but harms or unjustly restricts the rights or well-being of others. Terrorist and supremacist groups who believe in a cause and deliberately harm others to promote their ends fall into this category. Political scientist Barbara Kellerman (2004) describes this type of unethical leadership as evil. She explains that evil leaders and followers use pain as an instrument of power. The harm done to men, women, and children is severe rather than slight, and it can be physical, psychological, or both (Kellerman, 2004).

Other less visible or overtly harmful groups often form to preserve a way of life that favors them but denies rights and privileges to others in society. These groups are considered insular. "The leader and at least some followers minimize or disregard the health and welfare of 'the other'—that is, those outside the group or organization for which they are directly responsible" (Kellerman, 2004, p. 45).

Some neighborhood associations, for instance, form for the purpose of preserving the beauty, quality, safety, and market value of their communities. Generally, this kind of purpose applies only to a specific group and has little effect on others. Insularity occurs in cases where neighborhood associations like these refuse to allow access to housing or fair market price sales to residents of group homes, racial and ethnic minorities, gay and lesbian couples, or other individuals and families who also have respect for high-quality property maintenance and considerate neighborly practices.

Harm may also accrue to unintended victims of or parties injured by a well-intentioned purpose and group. For example, some organizations that engage in economic development efforts have been accused of harming the well-being of innocent victims of development by inadvertently weakening the social capital of a community, having funds intended for the community siphoned off by corrupt regimes, or not ensuring that community members receive appropriate financial compensation for their property or labor.

There are also situations where inspiring and ethical purposes are derailed by unethical, incompetent, or mentally imbalanced leaders or participants, and situations where individuals spiral downward into these circumstances over time. People often lose sight of their common purpose because of the influence of leaders or participants who overlook the common purpose due to their own incapacities, self-indulgent goals, or dysfunctions, as discussed extensively by sociologist Jean Lipman-Blumen in her book *The Allure of Toxic Leaders* (2004).

A classic example is Enron. Individual leaders and employees of Enron became self-indulgent, unethical, and engulfed by greed even though their organization began with an inspirational common purpose. Over time, with each wrong action, they lost sight of their moral anchor and purpose.

Though Enron is an obvious culprit, losing sight of the common purpose occurs more frequently than group or organizational members would like to admit. One respondent in the pilot test of our survey instrument commented, "Unfortunately [there is] a great disparity between practice and purpose." Mary Parker Follett (1949/1987) reminds us, "Loyalty to the invisible leader gives us the strongest possible bond of union." As a result, focus on the invisible leader must be at the forefront of an organization's decisions and actions. Leaders and participants must use ethical means and ends to achieve the common purpose. All members of the organization are held accountable for the common purpose and use of ethical means and ends. The organization's authorizing structures must be set up so that anyone can redirect people's attention back to the invisible leader.

Barbara Kellerman (2004) and sociologist Jean Lipman-Blumen (2005), in separate books on bad and toxic leadership, say that leaders and participants cocreate leadership. As a result, they are jointly responsible for its exercise and outcome. Kellerman asserts, "Leaders should be looked at only in tandem with their followers. Without followers nothing happens, including bad leadership" (p. 227). Lipman-Blumen adds,

> Accepting the responsibility to speak out is an important step in creating more democratic organizations that need able leaders at every level. And if confrontation doesn't yield the desired result, the liberated followers ultimately may have to consider ousting the toxic leader. (p. 239)

The points these scholars raise reiterate Follett's ideas about multiple leadership. Followers, as cocreators and implementers of the common purpose, must accept moral responsibility for the common purpose. They must avert the shadowy side of invisible leadership along with leaders or, when necessary, in opposition to leaders who stray from ethical purpose and action.

Opponents and Competitors

The common purpose of any group is rarely neutral to all groups outside their membership. There are groups who consciously oppose or compete with another group's common purpose. For many social movements, there are countermovement groups that are equally passionate about the cause or purpose for which they stand—for example, prochoice versus prolife, gay rights/gay marriage versus traditional families and marriage, or environmental versus wise use or antienvironmental movements. The countermovement groups feel strongly that their purpose is valid, ethical, and worthy of equal consideration.

Some groups or organizations with similar common purposes compete for the same or similar members, consumers, or participants. Examples include businesses, sports teams, and nonprofits such as universities or professional associations. These organizations want to benefit their members and supporters in the pursuit of their common purpose over others in the same field. In the case of both opposing and competing groups, the responsibility of leaders and followers when carrying out their common purpose is to act ethically toward people inside and outside the group or organization, and to extend this responsibility to opponents and collaborators in the same manner.

Other Ethical Issues

Groups and organizational members demonstrate that invisible leadership can strongly bind the members to each other. This positive circumstance can have negative consequences in certain situations—that is, it can potentially contribute to groupthink or in-group–out-group bias.

Groupthink

Psychologist Irving Janis defines *groupthink* as "a mode of thinking that people engage in when they are deeply involved in a cohesive ingroup, when the members' strivings for unanimity override their motivation to realistically appraise alternative courses of action" (as quoted in Forsyth, 2010, p. 337). Forsyth (2010) identifies several causes of groupthink based on Irving Janis's model, including cohesiveness, structural faults of the group or organization, and provocative situational contexts (pp. 341–342). Groups sometimes value their cohesiveness over critical thinking. They do not want to disagree, challenge assumptions, or risk losing friendships. The group's structure can prevent honest discourse and full evaluation of information. Groups can become isolated and removed from outside influence or information that is vital for effective decision making. Their leadership structure (who sets the agenda, how and when the formal leader's opinion is presented, and how final decisions are made) may stifle diverse opinions and increase conformity. The situation or context in which a group makes decisions can promote groupthink when the group must make high-stakes decisions under stress or threats from external sources, or when the group suffers from collective low self-esteem based on past mistakes.

Groupthink has contributed to morally irresponsible and avoidable negative consequences to other individuals and groups. The classic case of the *Challenger* disaster illustrates a situation where groupthink may have contributed to a decision to launch the space shuttle prematurely in poor weather conditions, and this resulted in the death of seven crew members. Groupthink can contribute to unethical decisions by executive groups that affect company members, investors, or the public; by political actors in nation-states concerning the welfare of their citizens or other countries; or by religious leaders or governing bodies in relation to the well-being of all segments of their congregations.

Groups engaged in invisible leadership can lessen their chances of succumbing to groupthink through limiting premature seeking of concurrence, correcting misperceptions and biases, using effective decision-making techniques (Forsyth, 2010, pp. 345–347), and fostering leaderful practice. Fostering leaderful practice, as discussed in Chapter 2, means that people work together as leaders for the common purpose. All members are equally valuable, and their contributions and ideas receive full consideration. This practice contributes to broader participation, diversity of thought, and lower probability of groupthink.

Group members, especially positional leaders, can promote environments where open inquiry and critical thinking thrive by welcoming diverse and dissenting ideas, criticism, and open discourse. Seeking unbiased thoughts and information from outsiders to the group or consultants expands the knowledge base and presents new options. Use of effective decision-making techniques—such as scenario building, analyzing alternative courses of action, considering intended and unintended consequences, and developing contingency plans—contributes to successful outcomes.

In-Group–Out-Group Bias

In-group–out-group bias is "the tendency to view one's group, its members, and its products more positively than other groups, their members, and their products" (Forsyth, 2010, p. 82). Although this bias can contribute to collective well-being and pride in belonging to the group, it can also contribute to distorted or discriminatory views of other groups, elitism, and unwarranted exclusionary practices. These factors can prevent the group from considering the value and contributions of other groups, and can cause it to disregard its ethical responsibility to those outside their group.

Approaches to overcoming in-group–out-group bias entail creating positive contact—that is, getting to know and interacting with the other group, developing supportive norms that facilitate egalitarian attitudes and discourage in-group–out-group judgments and comparisons, and collaborating with the other group in pursuit of common goals (Forsyth, 2010, p. 431–432). Collaboration in today's complex technological society has become essential for survival of many groups and organizations. Companies that were once fierce competitors are now collaborating. For instance, competing automobile companies have set up joint research and development teams and have jointly produced hybrid cars. Some small businesses join forces to attract large contracts. Nonprofit organizations now engage in collaborative fundraising. Even members of some rival gangs have collaborated to achieve community goals.

The Common Purpose
as Justification for Unethical Behavior

Certainly, a compelling and inspiring common purpose is central to the concept of invisible leadership. The strength, attraction, or importance of a common purpose, however, does not permit a group or leader to break generally held rules of moral behavior—such as telling the truth, keeping promises, or helping those in need—to attain the group's purpose (Price, 2008). Some groups and organizations with a compelling common purpose use the purpose to justify unethical behavior by leaders or group members. Hoyt, Price, and Emrick (2010) found that groups, and especially leaders of these groups, who exaggerate the importance of their group goals believe they are justified in deviating from moral requirements. They call this biased thought process the more-important-than-average (MITA) effect. The researchers conducted three studies where they found support for their hypothesis that people perceive their group goals as more important than other groups' goals, and in the minds of leaders, even more than members, this MITA rationale justifies unethical behavior to attain their group goals (Hoyt, Price, & Emrick, 2010, p. 401).

What types of unethical behavior did leaders and members think were permissible based on the MITA effect? Researchers asked participants to indicate their agreement with several statements using a scale ranging from 1 (strongly disagree) to 7 (strongly agree):

- In some circumstances, it would be alright for me to misrepresent the facts in order to achieve the goals of my organization;
- In some circumstances, it would be alright for me to misrepresent the facts in order to keep a key group member in the group;
- In some circumstances, it would be alright for me to misrepresent the facts in order to keep a rival group from doing better than us;
- When I have to misrepresent the facts, the goals of my organization serve as a justification for my actions;
- For the good of the group, I would be justified in doing what other people might think is unethical. (Hoyt, Price, & Emrick, 2010, p. 400)

Groups and their leaders are rarely justified in engaging in unethical behavior even when the common purpose that inspires invisible leadership is decidedly significant to the group and, in some cases, important for human and environmental well-being. Terry Price (2008) argues that moral exceptionalism—such as "lying to the Nazis to save the lives of Jews hiding inside your house"—occurs in extreme cases where heroic action is required (p. 216). Moral exceptionalism is not the behavior of everyday life and everyday leadership. Price does not suggest that everyday leadership is trivial or insignificant, but it does not warrant the type of extreme heroic leadership that may justify moral exceptionalism. His guiding principle provides direction for leaders and group members who engage in invisible leadership:

By differentiating organizational ends from the grand goals that may justify rule breaking in heroic leadership, everyday leaders are poised to work within the context of moral rules to carry out the individual and collective projects that characterize our day-to-day lives. (Price, 2008, p. 228)

Consequences of Invisible Leadership

Organizations and groups do not always know—nor can they always predict—the consequences of their dedicated pursuit of the common purpose. As Gini's earlier statement points out, at a minimum, we should intend no harm, respect the rights of all affected, not willfully or negligently trample on the rights and interests of others, and try to find a way to protect one person's individual rights and needs against and alongside the rights and needs of others. People will make mistakes or cause harm unintentionally even when they endeavor to act ethically, but the consequences of willful negligence or intentional harm are even more untenable.

On the website of BP Global, there are declarations of commitment to the environment, community, and managing the business, among other declarations throughout the site, although it is difficult to locate the company's central common purpose prominently in one place. Its website includes statements such as these:

> BP's code of conduct and values demonstrate our commitment to integrity, ethical values and legal compliance. Additionally, our commitment to competence is through having the right people with the right skills doing the right thing supported by our leadership framework.
>
> The GCE has established an operating style that sets direction for the company and places continual emphasis on our priorities of safety, people and performance. Delegation of authority, designed to make sure employees understand what is expected of them, is integral to this control environment. (BP, n.d.)

The company's 2009 annual report did not begin with a statement of BP's common purpose. Instead, former CEO Tony Hayward proclaimed in its opening executive review, "Achieving safe, reliable and compliant operations is our number one priority and the foundation stone for good business" (BP, 2009, p. 6).

After the catastrophic 2010 oil spill in the Gulf of Mexico, many people challenged BP's commitment to putting human and environmental safety first. The general public, residents of the Gulf states, and, most important, BP itself must ask, Did the company follow its invisible leader? Is the common purpose placed up front by every person in every undertaking? Is the common purpose ethical? Do company actors pursue ethical means and ends in the pursuit of the common goal? The consequences of this disaster were great—lives lost, businesses lost, families in financial ruin, and environmental devastation. There will be many subsequent investigations, commissions, and reports, but the consequences of this disaster demonstrated to the public and affected individuals that members of the company did not live up to their declarations of commitment and responsibility to the environment, community, and multiple stakeholders.

By examining the light, shadowy, and opposing sides of invisible leadership, we hope to guide groups and organizations toward moral purpose and actions. The intent of this chapter is to promote ethical means and ends in the development and practice of invisible leadership. A common purpose may be the motivating force for a small group or a large corporation, social movement, or collaboration among nation-states. Yet willingly bringing ourselves to the work of any common purpose requires that we hold ourselves accountable; that we consider the welfare of others inside and outside our group; and that our accountability begins with exposing, facing, and living up to the ethical responsibility of our actions.

In our next chapter, we transition from theoretical and ethical aspects of invisible leadership to research. We examine survey results from our study of companies and nonprofit organizations in the United States and several other countries.

References

Anderson, R. C., & White, R. A. (2009). *Confessions of a radical industrialist: Profits, people, purpose—doing business by respecting the earth.* New York, NY: St. Martin's Press.

BP. (2009). *BP annual report and accounts.* Retrieved July 13, 2010, from http://www.bp.com//assets/bp_internet/globalbp/globalbp_uk_english/set_branch/STAGING/common_assets/downloads/pdf/BP_Annual_Report_and_Accounts_2009.pdf

BP. (n.d.). *Governance.* Retrieved July 13, 2010, from http://www.bp.com/sectiongenericarticle.do?categoryId=9032649&contentId=7059900

Follett, M. P. (1949/1987). *Freedom & co-ordination: Lectures in business organization.* New York, NY: Garland.

Forsyth, D. R. (2010). *Group dynamics.* Belmont, CA: Wadsworth, Cengage Learning.

Gini, A. (2004). Moral leadership and business ethics. In J. B. Ciulla (Ed.), *Ethics, the heart of leadership* (2nd ed., pp. 25–43). Westport, CT: Praeger.

Hawken, P. (1993). *The ecology of commerce: A declaration of sustainability.* New York, NY: HarperBusiness.

Hoyt, C. L., Price, T. L., & Emrick, A. E. (2010). Leadership and the more-important-than-average effect: Overestimation of group goals and the justification of unethical behavior. *Leadership, 6*(4), 391–407.

Interface. (2008). *Mission/Vision: Interface's values are our guiding principles.* Retrieved July 12, 2010, from http://www.interfaceglobal.com/Company/Mission-Vision.aspx

Kellerman, B. (2004). Making meaning of being bad. In B. Kellerman (Ed.), *Bad leadership: What it is, how it happens, why it matters* (pp. 29–48). Boston, MA: Harvard Business School.

Lipman-Blumen, J. (2005). *The allure of toxic leaders: Why we follow destructive bosses and corrupt politicians—and how we can survive them.* New York, NY: Oxford University Press.

Price, T. L. (2004). Ethics: Overview. In G. R. Goethals, G. J. Sorenson, & J. M. Burns (Eds.), *Encyclopedia of leadership* (vol. 1, pp. 462–470). Thousand Oaks, CA: Sage.

Price, T. L. (2008). *Leadership ethics: An introduction.* New York, NY: Cambridge University Press.

Timberland. (n.d.). *CSR/Strategy.* Retrieved July 10, 2010, from http://www.timberland.com/corp/index.jsp?page=csr_strategy

4

Lighting the Path

The Invisible Leadership Study

We asked in Chapter 1, Does leadership involve a different dynamic from classic leader-centric concepts *when people already understand and are committed to an important purpose? When they know what needs to be done and willingly use their talents and skills to accomplish the work? When they hold themselves responsible and accountable for achieving the common purpose? When they sometimes seem to put the purpose ahead of their personal interests?* The answer is a resounding "Yes!"

These next two chapters are for those who want to drill down into the actual responses and data of our survey. We also encourage future research and want to provide a framework of our methodology and thinking.

Highlights From the Study

- 21 businesses and nonprofit organizations participated in the study.
- 415 participants (63% of those who received it) responded to the survey.
- We found an **invisible leadership factor**—seven subscales together formed this highly reliable scale.
- Participants said **the common purpose** was a top reason for joining and staying at their organization.
- 90% of participants agreed or strongly agreed that they were committed to achieving their organization's common purpose.
- 87% of participants accepted the common purpose as their own.
- 87% of participants agreed that the common purpose inspired them to contribute their best work.

Note: The authors would like to thank Donelson Forsyth and Crystal Hoyt for their invaluable contributions to this chapter.

- 79% of participants agreed that a **strong relationship bond formed among employees** working together on behalf of the common purpose.
- 93% of participants were willing to work in **either a leader *or* team member role** to accomplish the common purpose.

To examine the importance of purpose and the difference it makes in award-winning companies and organizations, we developed a survey instrument based on eight factors:

1. Self-selection/attraction,
2. Commitment or ownership,
3. Influence/inspiration to contribute,
4. Bond among participants,
5. Self-agency,
6. Taking action or leadership visibly (external to the organization) or invisibly (internal to the organization),
7. Rising above self-interest, and
8. Utilizing opportunities and resources.

The factors were derived by means of research, focus groups, and interviews with leaders, scholars, and our students. We developed questions for each factor, converted each question into a statement, and asked respondents to indicate the extent to which they agreed with each statement. These closed-ended questions (21 total) were combined with both open-ended (3) and demographic questions (7) resulting in a 31-item survey. The items were pilot-tested, and were found by methodologists to be highly reliable. The final survey was administered online. (See the Appendix for the survey instrument.)

Organizations in the Study

We invited organizations that had been named to the WorldBlu List of Most Democratic Workplaces—now or in the past—to participate in the survey. Traci Fenton, the founder of WorldBlu, describes the organization's mission as "championing the growth of democratically-run companies worldwide" (WorldBlu, n.d.). The organizations on the list are an array of diverse companies and nonprofit organizations engaged in consulting, media services, youth leadership development, volunteering, technology, manufacturing, telecommunications, and retail services from six countries. Our thinking was that organizations on the list represented environments where invisible leadership might thrive, since the first principle of WorldBlu's 10 principles of democratic organizations is *purpose and vision:*

A democratic organization is clear about why it exists (its purpose) and where it is headed and what it hopes to achieve (its vision). These act as its true North, offering guidance and discipline to the organization's direction. (Worldblu.com, n.d.)

The other principles—transparency, dialogue + listening, fairness + dignity, accountability, individual + collective, choice, integrity, decentralization, and reflection + evaluation (Worldblu.com, nd.)—seemed consistent with a climate of invisible leadership as we understood it.

Twenty-one of the 44 democratic companies and nonprofit workplaces participated in the survey, as depicted in Table 4.1. These organizations were among the smaller workforces on the WorldBlu list.[1] All 659 employees in the 21 organizations were invited to participate in the anonymous and confidential online survey. Among these employees, 415 responded, resulting in a strong response rate of 63%, a much higher rate than the average 53% (Baruch & Holtom, 2008). We had surmised that employees in democratic workplaces might be inspired to share information about their work at a higher rate than employees at a traditional organization, given the special context in which they work and their expanded involvement in the work and purpose. They did.

Organizational Purpose

The purposes of the organizations surveyed varied as widely as the organizations themselves (see Table 4.1). The most important aspect of each organization's purpose was that leaders and members clearly and effectively conveyed to others the characteristics that made their organization and its purpose special, unique, or significant. The purpose of these organizations, in most cases, was more than a mission statement that indicated what the organization did and why it existed. It was a "lived" purpose that infused meaning and importance into the day-to-day work and created a close bond or relationship among employees. Participants in the few organizations where there was no formal statement were still able to provide substantive responses about the purpose of their organization and the influence that purpose had on them and their coworkers. Yet some of these employees noted that a formal statement would help provide a clearer and more cohesive direction for building and sustaining a lived purpose in the organization.

---

[1]Representatives from most of the larger organizations expressed strong interest in the survey but declined to participate because of the numerous other internal and external surveys to which their employees were requested to respond.

Table 4.1   Reliability Statistics: Invisible Leadership Subscales

Company or Nonprofit	Product or Service[+]	Organization's Common Purpose	Location[**]
AIESEC International[*] aiesec.org	Youth leadership development		Rotterdam, Netherlands
Axiom News Services[*] axiomnews.ca	Media services for organizations		Peterborough, ON, Canada
BetterWorld Telecom[*] betterworldtelecom.com	Fixed line communications		Reston, VA
Brainpark[*] brainpark.com	Collaboration software		San Francisco, CA
Chroma Technology chroma.com	Optical filters and related products	Chroma Technology Corp. is a leading manufacturer of optical filters and related products that serve the scientific and technical communities. Our mission is to provide the best products and solutions for our customers' ever-changing needs. To that end we develop lasting relationships with our customers by providing applications expertise and exceptional customer service. Chroma is 100% employee-owned: each employee has a share of the responsibility for Chroma's success, and each earns a fair share of the rewards. We value the economic and social needs of the individual as well as	Rockingham, VT

Company	Service	Description	Location
		the needs of the company as a whole. This is how we create the committed, involved and healthy employee body that is key to achieving our mission. Chroma is an active and caring member of the community in which we live as well as the scientific and technical communities that we serve. We give back to these communities by providing jobs, offering financial support to local non-profit service agencies, sponsoring educational opportunities for students of science and technology, and promoting employee ownership.	
Dialog dialoggrp.com	Strategic marketing	MISSION: To Extend the Practice of Marketing and Management by Helping Leading Companies Grow their Revenue, People and Capability	Austin, TX
DreamHost* dreamhost.com	Web hosting		Brea, CA
Equal Exchange equalexchange.coop	Fairly traded and organic food products	Equal Exchange has created *Big Change* since 1986. Our founders envisioned a food system that empowers farmers and consumers, supports small farmer co-ops, and uses	West Bridgewater, MA

(Continued)

Table 4.1 Continued

Company or Nonprofit	Product or Service[+]	Organization's Common Purpose	Location[**]
		sustainable farming methods. They started with fairly traded coffee from Nicaragua and didn't look back.	
		Today, we continue to find new and powerful ways to build a better food system. We partner with co-operatives of farmers who provide high-quality organic coffees, teas, chocolates, bananas, olive oil, and snacks from all over the world.	
		We invite you to join us. Together we can create stronger local communities, a more just food system and a healthier planet.	
Future Considerations futureconsiderations .com	Management consultancy	Vision: A sustainable and abundant world in which all elements co-exist and develop in harmony. Purpose: To enable the world's leaders, institutions and systems to evolve, and to influence the great challenges of the time. Values: Authenticity Care Courage Learning Integrity	London, UK

Glassdoor glassdoor.com	Internet career and job site	To become the world's most trusted community for workplace and career information.	Sausalito, CA
Haiti Partners haitipartners.org	Education and community development	To help Haitians change Haiti through education for **Students** **Teachers** **Leaders** **Disciples**	Port-au-Prince, Haiti and Vero Beach, FL
I Love Rewards iloverewards.com	Online incentive program software	To Change the Way the World Works	Toronto, ON, Canada
Innovation Partners International innovationpartners.com	Specialized consulting services	Innovation Partners International is the world's leading strength-based consulting firm. Our work is done with a difference—we focus on what you're good at, your aspirations and opportunities. We leverage your strengths to identify and implement needed innovations in areas that make a difference to your human and business outcomes. We bring our innovative positive change model to life, both in what we offer our clients and in the everyday fabric of our	Portland, ME

(Continued)

Table 4.1   Continued

Company or Nonprofit	Product or Service+	Organization's Common Purpose	Location**
		lives. In doing so, we are proving a viable approach to organizational excellence, where individuals thrive, businesses flourish, and legacies are born.	
Menlo Innovations menloinnovations.com	Software design and development	Our goal since 2001 is to return the joy to one of the most unique endeavors in the history of mankind: inventing software! Menlo Innovations is a for-hire custom software design and development firm located in Ann Arbor, MI. Our mission is to "end human suffering in the world as it relates to technology™." We do this by focusing on three key stakeholders in our industry: **Software project sponsors** who traditionally have had little hope of steering projects to a successful conclusion before money and executive patience is exhausted. **End users of the software**, who, far too often, have no voice at all in the design, yet must live every day with the decisions of people they have never met.	Ann Arbor, MI

Company	Description		Location
		The software teams themselves, who typically labor under years of overtime, missed vacations and family celebrations, broken relationships and unrealistic expectations only to have the projects they work on never see the light of day.	Kuala Lumpur, Malaysia
Mindvalley* mindvalley.com	Publishing of personal growth products		
Nearsoft nearsoft.com	Software product development services	Mission Partner with our clients to deliver superior project development and consulting services that produce innovative software products with a measurable return on investment in long-term relationships. Our Vision Become one of the top three Mexican companies known for quality and cost/benefit outsourcing for the American market. Become the best place to work and develop professionally, personally and financially speaking for its associates.	San Jose, CA
NixonMcInnes nixonmcinnes.co.uk	Social consultancy	Our mission at NixonMcInnes is to better enable society's organisations to evolve,	Brighton, UK

(Continued)

Table 4.1 Continued

Company or Nonprofit	Product or Service[+]	Organization's Common Purpose	Location[**]
		harnessing the latent positive power in the relationships between them, their people, their consumers and their wider ecosystems.	
		We do this by working with clients to uncover, prototype and embed new working practices and technologies, which advance them in their journey to becoming a Social Business.	
		An important additional contributor is using our own open, democratic culture as an example and test bed for exploring these new working practices and technologies.	
Rypple[*] rypple.com	Internet performance management platform		Toronto, ON, Canada
sweetriot[*] sweetriot.com	Fair trade, all-natural chocolate products		New York, NY
TakingITGlobal[*] tigweb.org	Internet social network for global issues		Toronto, ON, Canada
UniversalGiving universalgiving.org	Web-based philanthropy and volunteering	"To Create a World Where Giving and Volunteering Are a Natural Part of Everyday Life."™	San Francisco, CA

[+]Information summarized from each organization's website.

[*]The organization did not provide a formal common purpose.

[**]Information taken from Worldblu's website: http://worldblu.com/awardee-profiles/2010.php.

Demographics

Most organizations in the survey represented the business sector (72.4%); nonprofit or nongovernmental organizations composed a smaller segment (13.5%) of participants (see Table 4.2).[2] The majority of respondents described their affiliation with the organization as employees or team members (57.1%), whereas managers and executives represented 16.5% and 17.1%, respectively (see Table 4.3).

Table 4.2   Percentage of Respondents From Each Organizational Sector

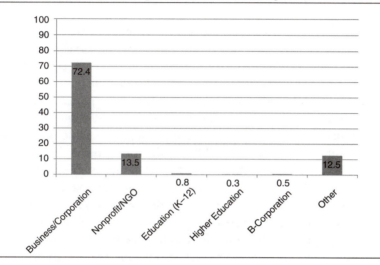

Table 4.3   Percentage of Respondents From Each Employee Category

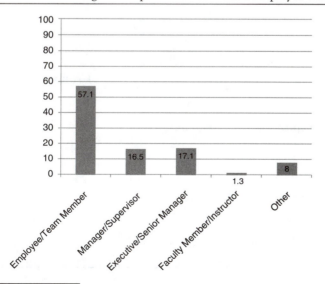

---

[2]Percentages and numbers of participants throughout the chapter are based on the respondents who answered each question. Some respondents skipped questions.

The majority of respondents were full-time employees (79.4%); a smaller percentage of respondents were part-time and volunteer employees (13.0%); and other affiliations represented 7.7%.[3] They were employed an average of 3.27 years (median 2.0 years), and there were slightly more men (53.4%) than women (46.6%); the average age was 32.9 years (median age of 29).

The Invisible Leadership Factor

All of the subscales except for the self-selection/attraction subscale were assessed using Likert-type items. In this type of psychometric scale, respondents indicate their level of agreement with statements relevant to the question or construct of interest. The self-selection/attraction subscale asked participants to indicate the main reasons they joined and stayed at their organizations. Analyses of the Likert-type items from all seven sub-scales revealed that together they formed a highly reliable scale of invisible leadership (Cronbach's α = .90). Furthermore, the items within each subscale cohered well, as indicated by the reliability of the individual sub-scales in Table 4.4. Importantly, the data are correlational and not causal. Correlational studies can suggest that there is a relationship between two variables, but they cannot prove that a change in one variable causes a change in another variable. Other hidden factors may be at work; however, the correlations in this study were very strong, and their relationships with each other were also strong.

Table 4.4   Reliability Statistics: Invisible Leadership Subscales

Items	Cronbach's Alpha
Commitment	.73
Influence and inspiration to contribute	.77
Bonding	.75
Self-agency	.65
Take action visibly or invisibly	.64
Rise above self-interest	.74
Take advantage of or utilize opportunities and resources	.77

---

[3]Percentage may total slightly more than 100% due to rounding.

Subscale Results

All seven of the subscales were significantly and positively correlated with each other, with subscale correlation coefficients r ranging from .29 to .62 (see Table 4.5). Additionally, the overall invisible leadership scale correlated strongly with each subscale.

Table 4.5   Correlations Among Subscales

Variable	1	2	3	4	5	6	7	8
1. **Commitment** Individual's commitment to/ownership of the purpose	—	.54	.51	.49	.50	.42	.33	.79
2. **Influence** Influence of common purpose on person to contribute their best effort or work		—	.55	.62	.41	.39	.60	.82
3. **Bond** Acting on behalf of common purpose creates strong shared bond			—	.52	.44	.39	.42	.73
4. **Agency** Common purpose generates self-agency to take action (leadership)				—	.47	.35	.51	.76
5. **Visible/Invisible** Willingness to take action (leadership) visibly or invisibly on behalf of purpose					—	.38	.29	.70
6. **Self-Interest** Willingness to rise above self-interest to achieve the common purpose						—	.39	.62
7. **Opportunities** Taking advantage or making use of resources/opportunities to achieve purpose							—	.68
8. **Overall Invisible Leadership Scale**								—

Note: All correlations are significant at the .001 level (2-tailed).

Self-Selection/Attraction

We wanted to determine whether the common purpose of a company or nonprofit influences individuals to join an organization (self-selection or choice). Among the top four reasons employees joined their organization, the common purpose ranked highest for almost 30% of employees, followed by 25.8% of employees who joined for professional growth or career opportunities, 13.3% who joined for their organization's work environment, and 8.2% who joined because of the organization's team members or coworkers (see Table 4.6).

Only 5.1% of respondents said they joined the organization for its compensation (pay and benefits). This contrasts with a global study of organizations produced by Kenexa Research Institute (2010) of a representative sample of workers surveyed by WorkTrends in which salary and compensation ranks first in terms of recruitment motivators.

They come, but do they stay? The reasons employees stay with their organizations vary somewhat from the reasons they join (see Table 4.7). The number of employees who chose the common purpose (25.6%) and professional growth or career opportunities (24.1%) as reasons to stay was slightly less than the number of employees who chose these reasons for joining a company, but they were the top two reasons employees stayed. Work environment and team members or coworkers increased in importance for respondents remaining at their organizations (23.7% and 13.2%, respectively).

Table 4.6   The main reason I joined my organizations is its

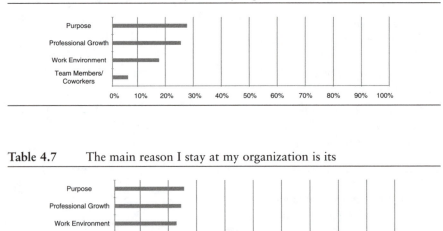

Table 4.7   The main reason I stay at my organization is its

Commitment to or Ownership of the Purpose

We asked several questions to determine the individual's commitment to the common purpose. Table 4.8 indicates a majority of respondents agreed or strongly agreed that they were highly committed to achieving their organization's purpose (90.4%), and they believed their coworkers were highly committed to the purpose (84.9%). Individuals accepted the organization's purpose as their own (87.2%), and many respondents indicated that their personal passion aligned with the organization's purpose (77.5%).

Influence or Inspiration to Contribute

Did the common purpose influence or inspire individuals to contribute their best effort or work (skills, abilities, or talents) to achieve that purpose? The results in Table 4.9 show that the organization's purpose provides strong inspiration for respondents (86.6 %) and their coworkers (82.2%) to contribute their best work. While a majority of individuals indicated that their organizations acknowledged employees for their outstanding work toward achieving the purpose (69.8%), an even higher percentage

Table 4.8   Commitment to/Ownership of the Purpose: Percentage of Respondents Who Agree or Strongly Agree

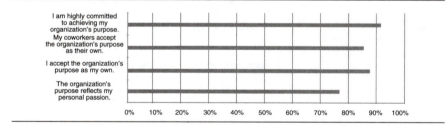

Table 4.9   Influence or Inspiration to Contribute Best Effort/Work: Percentage of Respondents Who Agree or Strongly Agree

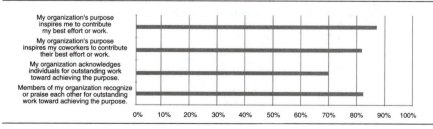

of respondents said that coworkers recognized or praised each other for outstanding work toward the purpose (82.2%). There was clear alignment to purpose and to each other's role in sustaining it.

Bond Among Participants

We examined whether working together on behalf of a common purpose created a strong shared bond among organizational members (see Table 4.10). Most respondents (78.5%) agreed that their joint work toward the common purpose created a strong bond or relationship among employees, and 73.5% reported a strong relationship with members of the organization.

Self-Agency

In addition to asking about a bond around the common purpose, we wondered whether individuals had self-agency to take action (leadership) to achieve the purpose. Table 4.11 shows that respondents believe they have the power to act on behalf of their organization's purpose (78.3%), and they believe their coworkers can act in support of the purpose (72.4%).

Table 4.10   Bond Among Participants: Percentage of Respondents Who Agree or Strongly Agree

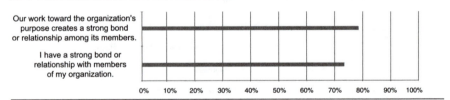

Table 4.11   Self-Agency: Percentage of Respondents Who Agree or Strongly Agree

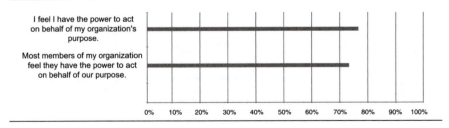

Taking Action Visibly or Invisibly

We wanted to know if individuals would work in either a leader or team member (effective follower) role to achieve the organization's purpose (see Table 4.12). Most respondents (92.4%) were willing to work in either role to accomplish the purpose.

There were several questions related to the respondents' need for visibility (external to the organization) when they worked on behalf of the common purpose. In other words, does visibility outside the organization matter to employees when they work on behalf of the purpose? Most respondents (86.1%) indicated that they were willing to work in a role that was not visible to people outside the organization to achieve the common purpose, although almost as great a percentage (77.7%) were willing to work in a visible role to achieve the organization's purpose. This finding contrasts with much of the research in this field, which shows that leadership opportunities in traditionally visible roles are often a major incentive for good employees to remain with an organization.

Table 4.12   Taking Action Visibly or Invisibly: Percentage of Respondents Who Agree or Strongly Agree

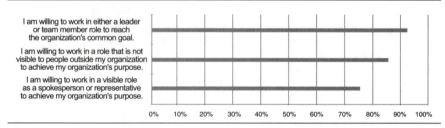

Rising Above Self-Interest

We asked if individuals were willing to rise above self-interest (e.g., volunteer or spend extra time, give up personal events, or risk harm) to achieve their organization's common purpose. Almost 64% of respondents were willing to place the common purpose above their immediate self-interest when necessary, and 63% thought their coworkers were also willing to sacrifice for the common purpose (see Table 4.13 on following page).

Table 4.13   Rising Above Self-Interest: Percentage of Respondents Who Agree
or Strongly Agree

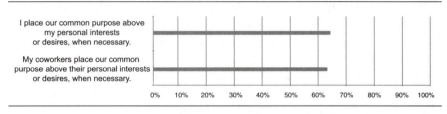

Taking Advantage of or Utilizing Opportunities and Resources

Opportunities and resources are essential for achieving any common purpose. Did coworkers care enough about the organization and its purpose to find resources to achieve the purpose? You bet! Members of these exemplary organizations took advantage of (or made the most of) opportunities and resources to advance the common purpose. Table 4.14 shows that most respondents (76.8%) thought their coworkers used key opportunities—such as suitable occasions, decisive moments, or turning points—to advance the purpose, and 77.6% answered that their coworkers knew how to find financial, human, or technological resources their organizations needed to achieve the common purpose.

Table 4.14   Taking Advantage of or Utilizing Opportunities and Resources:
Percentage of Respondents Who Agree or Strongly Agree

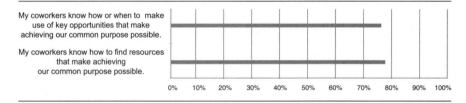

Factor Analysis

What Is Factor Analysis?

Factor analysis is a data reduction technique. It attempts to identify a small set of factors that represents the underlying relationships among a group of related variables (Pallant, 2007, pp. 179, 185).

We conducted a factor analysis to determine the unique factors associated with invisible leadership in our survey. They encompassed most of the subscales. We labeled these factors *collective capacity, internalized purpose, role flexibility,* and *purpose-inspired dedication and accountability* (see Table 4.15).

Table 4.15   Factor Analysis

Factors	Factor Loadings
Factor 1—Collective Capacity	
Q9 My organization's purpose inspires my coworkers to contribute their best effort or work.	.54
Q10 My organization acknowledges individuals for outstanding work toward achieving the purpose.	.68
Q11 Members of my organization recognize or praise each other for outstanding work.	.76
Q12 Our work toward the organization's purpose creates a strong bond or relationship among its members.	.53
Q15 Most members of my organization feel they have the power to act on behalf of our purpose.	.64
Q21 My coworkers know how or when to make use of key opportunities (occasions, decisive moments, turning points) that make achieving our common purpose possible.	.67
Q22 My coworkers know how to find resources (financial, human, or technological) that make achieving our common purpose possible.	.63
Factor 2—Internalized Purpose	
Q4 I am highly committed to achieving my organization's purpose.	.54
Q6 I accept the organization's purpose as my own.	.78
Q7 The organization's purpose reflects my personal passion.	.67
Factor 3—Role Flexibility	
Q16 I am willing to work in either a leader or team member role to reach the organization's common goal.	.66
Q18 I am willing to work in a visible role as a spokesperson or representative to achieve my organization's purpose.	.60
Factor 4—Purpose-Inspired Dedication and Accountability	
Q19 I place our common purpose above my personal interests or desires, when necessary.	.69
Q20 My coworkers place our common purpose above their personal interests or desires, when necessary.	.74

The first factor, collective capacity, involves

- Members contributing their best efforts to the shared work of the group (the common purpose),
- Recognition of praiseworthy work toward the purpose by peers and the organization,
- Creation of strong bonds among members fostered by their mutual focus on the purpose, and
- Use of self-agency by members to act on behalf of collective aims, or to make use of opportunities and obtain resources for the common purpose.

The second factor, internalized purpose, involves members seeing the purpose as a cause for which they are willing to invest considerable personal effort, or seeing the common purpose as a reflection of their own aspiration or passion. The third factor, role flexibility, is the willingness of members to serve the purpose in any needed capacity (leader, team member, or visible representative). The fourth factor, purpose-inspired dedication and accountability, entails accepting personal responsibility (or doing whatever it takes) to achieve the common purpose because the purpose is inherently worthwhile.

There could be several reasons why these four factors were extracted rather than all seven factors (excluding self-selection or attraction). The items are fairly similar and have considerable overlap. There is a restricted response range, and most respondents answered "agree" or "strongly agree," probably due to the highly engaged organizations in which they work. While our intention was to focus this first study on highly engaged organizations, a wider variety of organizations—both traditional and nontraditional—will need to be included in future studies.

Ancillary Analyses

We conducted several ancillary analyses in addition to testing key questions concerning invisible leadership. We wanted to know whether there were differences among respondents based on organization type, length of time with the organization, respondent's sex, and connection to the organization. The results of our analyses indicated statistically significant differences for three of these four factors and no differences for one factor.

Organization Type

Our analysis compared for-profit and nonprofit organizations using a multivariate analysis of variance. There were two significant effects: *On the self-interest subscale, which measured willingness to rise above self-interest to achieve the common purpose, respondents from nonprofit organizations reported higher levels of agreement than respondents from for-profit organizations* (*p* = .06). This result may be due to the emphasis nonprofit organizations place on achieving their purpose, while for-profit organizations have a dual emphasis of meeting their purpose and making a profit for investors.

Conversely, *on the opportunities subscale, which measured the extent to which employees took advantage of or made use of resources and opportunities to achieve the common purpose, respondents from nonprofit organizations reported lower levels of agreement than respondents from for-profit organizations* (*p* = .01). This response may reflect the ongoing struggle of many nonprofits to commit adequate time to finding and acquiring resources and opportunities due to lack of adequate personnel or experience.

Length of Time With the Organization

Next, to examine whether the length of time individuals have been with an organization is associated with invisible leadership, we conducted correlational analyses between the length of time the participants had been with their organization and all seven subscales of invisible leadership. *Respondents' length of time with an organization was significantly correlated with four subscales—bond, visible/invisible, influence, and opportunities. Members who had been with the organization longer scored higher on shared bond (that is, acting on behalf of the common purpose creates strong shared bond)* (*r* = .15, *p* = .005). We surmise that coworkers who had been with the organization longer develop close work relationships and friendships while working together toward a common purpose. (See Chapter 5 for respondents' comments about shared bonds.) *These respondents with longer tenure also scored higher on the visible/invisible scale, which measured willingness to take action (leadership) visibly/externally or invisibly/ internally on behalf of purpose* (*r* = .16, *p* = .002). Respondents with longer time in the organization may feel confident enough about their experience and capabilities to move easily between visible and invisible roles, and they may have been founding or early members of the organization who know all aspects of the organization.

Respondents who had been with the organization longer reported lower scores on influence—that is, influence of the common purpose on individuals to contribute their best effort or work (r = −.15, p = .005). While the reason for these lower scores is not fully apparent, they may view the common purpose as consistent with their own personal mission or passion and not as a separate incentive to contribute their best work. Comments from a few respondents indicated that they were intrinsically motivated to contribute their best work apart from the common purpose (see Chapter 5). In other words, they were self-motivated toward doing their best work and did not need motivation from another source.

Respondents who had been with the organization longer likewise reported lower scores on opportunities (that is, taking advantage of or making use of resources and opportunities to achieve the common purpose) (r = −14, p = .009). This response may be attributed to the wording of the items: "My coworkers know how or when to make use of key opportunities (occasions, decisive moments, turning points) that make achieving our common purpose possible," and "My coworkers know how to find resources (financial, human, or technological) that make achieving our common purpose possible." Longer-term employees may feel they are more capable of responding to key opportunities or finding resources than their coworkers. In future versions of the survey, this item may be reworded to say, *we* or *I* rather than *my coworkers.*

Respondents' Sex

Both men (53.4%) and women (46.6%) were well represented in the study. An analysis using the respondents' sex *revealed no differences between women and men in responses on the seven subscales of invisible leadership.* This finding could suggest that invisible leadership fosters similar commitment, participation, and achievement by women and men in their work environment due to the organization's focus on the common purpose, and deemphasizes differences based on nonessential factors. This finding was somewhat surprising in light of women's tendency toward more invisible roles in society as a whole. Perhaps organizations with compelling common purpose elicit more visibility from women than would otherwise be the case.

Connection to the Organization

We conducted analyses to see whether there were differences in responses between positional leaders and members/employees. We created two categories—leaders (combined executives and managers) and employees—and conducted a multivariate analysis of variance on all subscales. *Leaders reported higher levels of agreement than employees on all subscales ($p \le .001$) except for the influence and opportunities subscales, where there were no significant differences ($ps > .50$).* A similar analysis using the positional leaders versus members/employees variable *on the combined invisible leadership scale similarly revealed that leaders scored higher than employees ($p < .001$).*

Finally, we conducted an analysis similar to the previous one where we looked at executives, managers, and employees separately. The graphs show a stepwise pattern where, predictably, managers are somewhere in between executives and employees. This difference between managers and executives is reliably significant only on the visible/invisible subscale (willingness to take action or leadership visibly or invisibly on behalf of purpose), where *managers have higher scores than employees, and executives have higher scores than managers.* Using the combined invisible leadership scale, there is *a nonsignificant trend ($p < .13$) where executives report higher willingness than managers to take leadership visibly or invisibly, and the differences between employees and each of the two leader groups are significant* (managers: $p < .05$; executives: $p < .001$).

These differences between leaders and members may support Kelley's (1988) idea that leader and follower are different but equal "roles" that encompass different responsibilities on behalf of the group for achieving the common purpose. Higher scores by positional leaders in this study on the overall invisible leadership scale could reflect these differences in responsibility that the role of leader places on its occupants. For example, when we asked if respondents were willing to work in a role that was not visible to people outside their organization to achieve its purpose, one person responded, "My role is to be the 'public face' of the company." We interpret this to mean the role of leader carries the responsibility to serve as the public face of the organization regardless of the occupant's preference to be seen or unseen.

Keep in mind that each organization has a different product, different positional leaders and members, and different organizational and, in some cases, national cultures. Yet the findings of our study suggest that no matter the sector or the gender or the role a person occupies—or the country—the power and utility of invisible leadership is unmatched by other factors. It is the "space between" that makes all things possible and exciting.

Next we will turn to the people who work for these extraordinary companies and organizations and hear their own words about the power of invisible leadership.

References

Baruch, Y., & Holtom, B. C. (2008). Survey response rate levels and trends in organizational research. Human Relations, 61(8), 1139-1160.

Kelley, R. E. (1988). In praise of followers. *Harvard Business Review, 66*(6), 142–148.

Kenexa Research Institute. (2010). *Why do people join organizations?* Executive Summary No. 23. Retrieved August 20, 2012, from http://www.kenexa.com/getattachment/a83cc13f-6c39–4e16-a673–5f51e4398414/Why-Do-People-Join-Organizations.aspx

Pallant, J. (2007). *SPSS survival manual.* Berkshire, UK: McGraw-Hill/Open University Press.

Worldblu.com. (n.d.). *Freedom by design: The Worldblu 10 principles of organizational democracy.* Retrieved June 18, 2011, from http://worldblu.com/democratic-design/principles.php

5

Seeing the Unseen

Experiences With Invisible Leadership

Individuals in our survey offered valuable examples and information about how leaders and members generate invisible leadership in their companies and nonprofit organizations. In this section, we share the words and experiences of many of the respondents that show how this phenomenon works.

Self-Selection and Attraction

People who experience invisible leadership in their organizations describe it in compelling terms. Many survey respondents expressed heartfelt sentiments about their organization's purpose as a primary reason for their attraction to, selection of, and commitment to staying in the organization:

- The mission is a core driver as to why I am passionate about the work I do, and why I feel I am leading a bigger movement and contributing to meaningful work.
- I sacrificed short-term benefits (including higher salary and more free time) to join [my organization] and make this dream a reality for millions of people.
- If this organization did not have this purpose, I would not stay here.

The environment of these organizations seemed to promote professional growth and career development as a result of meaningful work responsibilities, highly participatory environments, and supportive coworkers.

These factors were attractive incentives, even though many organizations in the study did not have the typical vertical career paths of larger or more traditionally structured organizations. Environment and team members or coworkers were important not only in attracting respondents, they became more valuable as members remained in the organization. The longer members and workers stayed with an organization, the more important the company's or nonprofit's work environment became to them. In our survey, the percentage of workers who reported that the work environment was "important" or "very important" was 13.3% for the newest arrivals, and 23.7% for those who had been at an organization the longest. Similarly, the percentage of workers who reported that valued coworkers were "important" or "very important" was 8.2% for the newest workers and 13.2% for those with the longest tenure.

A fourth of the survey respondents joined their organizations for professional growth and career opportunities apart from or in addition to the common purpose. One respondent commented, "I think it's a good purpose, but I'm mostly looking for experience and the support that coworkers provide." Another commented, "I agree [that I am highly committed to achieving my organization's purpose] since this way I can get to where I want to go and learn." One other respondent said that commitment to the purpose "will help me grow professionally—tied in with stock options as well."

Ownership or Commitment to the Purpose

The common purpose varied widely among the 21 organizations that we surveyed, as indicated in Chapter 4. One key to commitment was the idea of purpose as a daily "lived" experience by members of the organization. Respondents' comments included the following:

- We are very purpose driven, and I think the strength of the relationships that hold us together in pursuit of that purpose is a result of us living that purpose ourselves. We are in continual conversation about our strengths and how we can build on them, on our development as leaders and contributors to our field.
- We are passionate about what we do at all levels of the company—from the lowest to the highest—and we want everything to be the best that it can be. When it's not, we're all frustrated by it. It's nice to feel part of a HUGE team working toward a common goal.
- I've stayed here for 8+ years because I believe we are making an impact by carrying out [our] mission (purpose).
- All over the world, human rights are ignored. That's why I am highly committed and involved—to achieve [my organization's] purpose.

Others provided insight into how companies bring about and sustain this lived commitment. One respondent stated that members are "inducted" into the company's purpose "right away from their first weeks." Another said, "Rigorous hiring ensures that nearly everyone on board is very engaged in the company." An organization member highlighted the fact that "this purpose debate is kept alive in our organization by regular reviews and dialogues and this enables a constant reconnecting with it and the ability to verify it as part in the work I do." These comments point out that new members need to be incorporated into the life of the purpose, and continuing members need to engage each other frequently in dialogue about topics, questions, and concerns involving the purpose.

Though the majority of individuals (90.4%) reported strong commitment to the purpose, some respondents identified problems that contributed to a weakened or diminished commitment. One person stated that commitment to the purpose would be easier if "the purpose were more concise and concrete," even though the respondent generally agreed with the organization's philosophy and attitude. Some people identified a "disconnect" between the organization's stated purpose and the lived behaviors in the organization, and they disagreed with the way the purpose was being implemented: "To some extent, I believe in what we are trying to achieve, not so much in the way we are doing it." Another indicated that change in the organization can bring about movement away from the purpose or create distrust among members: "Things at this company have changed a lot. There is a lot of distrust now. . . ." These comments remind leaders and members to ensure that the organization's common purpose is clear and tangible, to build processes and practices that align the stated purpose with individual and collective behaviors, and to create processes or practices that are fully compatible with the purpose and values of the organization. Attention to the clarity of organizational purpose, alignment of behaviors, transparency, and sustaining trust become even more critical priorities for positional leaders when there is a shift or change in organizational purpose or direction.

Commitment to the common purpose also fostered positive self-interest and development of individual members in many organizations in the survey. We reported that 84.9% of respondents saw their organization's purpose as their own, and 77.5% expressed that their organization's purpose aligned with their personal passion. Their responses suggest that the common purpose embodies certain personal or intrinsic aspirations of many members:

- I feel my personal sense of purpose and the organization's are closely linked, to the point of being identical.
- This purpose is closely connected to my own personal goals and ambitions.

- My personal passion is more connected with the development of young people and the power of youth to drive change, which is much connected with the organization's purpose.

Two other themes emerged from the comments about whether respondents accepted their organization's purpose as their own, and whether the organization's purpose reflected their personal passion. The first theme focused on the emergence of personal passion as an ongoing or developmental process. One person commented that the organization's purpose was "maybe not the final goal of my life, but something which I stand for." Another respondent said, "In this stage of my life I do [accept the organization's purpose as my own]. Who knows where my future will lead me though." Another said, "The organization helps me find my passion, still on the way."

The second theme highlights that individuals can have multiple passions in their lives. For example, the responses included these two: "I do not feel that this purpose is mutually exclusive with other purposes and professional goals in my life," and "it may not be my ultimate goal in life to help the company achieve everything we want it to, but, while I'm here, I'll rock out as best as I can!" Still, one respondent rejected the whole idea of comingling personal passion with the organization's purpose—"My work and who I am are separate."

These themes emphasize the diverse perspectives that exist among members of organizations. They suggest that some members have personal purposes and passions that may not be the same as the organizations', and they can still be effective organizational contributors. The role of organizational leaders and members is to identify and cultivate the elements that contribute to and sustain these individuals as effective contributors to the common purpose.

Influence or Inspiration to Contribute

The common purpose clearly inspired organization members to contribute their best work. Comments by respondents indicated that the influence of their team members or coworkers played a vital supporting role. Several respondents expressed similar thoughts: "I feel like I'm letting the whole team down if I don't give my best. And bring the best out in others!" "My coworkers inspire me to contribute my best effort or work." Additionally, a few respondents cited other intrinsic motivations as reasons for their drive to achieve the purpose: "The purpose influences me, but I think my work ethic is naturally strong," and "my work ethic is what motivates me to contribute my best effort to my workplace."

In contrast, other respondents observed that the absence of coworkers had a dampening effect on their work effort. Two comments illustrated this frustration:

- I work in a home regional office and find that missing out on coworker interaction, as well as other issues, prevent me from actually putting forth my best effort.
- While the purpose of [company name] is inspiring, at times the work environment can feel silo-ed and autonomous, which has an adverse reaction on me—making me feel isolated and cut off from my coworkers and thus the energy that inspires great work.

Problems not addressed by formal leaders also contributed to dampening the work efforts of respondents:

- The current state [of my organization] leads me to question whether I do contribute my best effort, as I often find myself getting slightly demotivated or think that nobody cares.
- It has to be more than the purpose. It's hard to stay motivated when there is no respect or collaboration.
- I don't always feel that they are doing the best job because they spend a lot more time with discussions than with action.

Most respondents felt that the common purpose also inspired their coworkers to contribute their best work: "I feel I am part of a team that is as equally committed as I am." "'Make your partner look good' is a common phrase around here." Yet the percentage of respondents who agreed or strongly agreed that their coworkers were inspired by the purpose to contribute their best work was lower than those who agreed or strongly agreed that they themselves were inspired by the purpose. Respondents were somewhat hesitant to speculate about what inspired their coworkers, or were simply unsure:

- It [the common purpose] should [inspire coworkers' best work]. I don't know if it does.
- I guess so, even though some might not be as enthusiastic about it as I am.
- I'm not sure to what extent I can speak for others—it seems to be the case for the majority, but we're all individuals!

Are individuals in these organizations acknowledged for their outstanding work toward achieving the common goal? We wondered why only 69.8% agreed or strongly agreed that their organization acknowledged the outstanding work of individuals. The respondents' comments indicated two reasons.

First, many of their organizations recognized teamwork more than individual work, which reflects their collaborative environments. They revealed, "The organization works very hard to acknowledge outstanding team work over individual accomplishment," and "we don't want an individual hero so much as someone who helps the team achieve goals. We work in pairs." One respondent explained the benefit of their team recognition approach: "Our CEO definitely gives credit where credit is due, but focuses a lot on a community/shared effort. I like that a lot more than working on the success of yourself. It promotes more company growth."

Some organizations have developed systems or programs for recognition of outstanding work by fellow coworkers; others use more informal, yet consistent, approaches. They are a mixture of intrinsic and extrinsic rewards:

- We have a monthly voting system where the entire crew will allocate 100 points across the name list of employees. The top 5 people who get the highest amount of points will be openly appreciated by the entire crew. It's a pleasant feeling to be appreciated by everyone. On top of all the appreciation, there is an added bonus for that month for all of the winners.
- Whenever anyone achieves a win, we all cheer that on. Positive reinforcement is a daily part of this environment. As is team work and support for one another to be the best they can be.
- We have monthly community awesomeness awards that both recognize outstanding work as well as give additional compensation.
- We use public recognition (kudos) to recognize others' work. Our organization has a kind of culture of appreciation, where positive feedback is commonly given informally for good work.

The second reason for this difference in response rate was omission or neglect by formal leaders in the organization. Respondents' comments included these:

- It would be awesome if upper management would remember to give the lower ranks a verbal pat on the back sometimes, though.
- I think that this [recognition for good work] happens now and then, but many people are overlooked or forgotten for the accomplishments they've achieved.
- We could do this better. Sometimes I don't think we applaud people's efforts because we take it as a given that we're all here for at least one of multiple purposes . . . and therefore we expect everyone to work hard.

Eighty-two percent of all respondents agreed or strongly agreed that coworkers, rather than managers or leaders, recognized each other for outstanding work toward achieving the common goal. We speculate that survey participants responded somewhat unfavorably to our use of the word *individuals* (i.e., "my organization acknowledges individuals for outstanding work toward achieving the purpose") instead of *team members*, because there is a genuine emphasis on mutual support and teamwork rather than individual achievement in these organizations. Respondents were enthusiastic in their descriptions of coworker recognition:

- I have never seen an organization where employees take ownership in the way they do here. Each person takes personal responsibility for recognizing others for their achievements.
- We have another system in place that helps us all send thank you notes/appreciations/and congratulation notes to each other. It really helps boost morale when you see that your work has helped people within the company.
- We use our staff meetings for this plus our Wall of Accomplishment.
- Team members (peers) are the primary source of recognizing individual contributions.

There were also cases where peer and organization recognition was lacking:

- I think the intention is there, but the reality often gets lost in chasing more tangible—and more short-term—business results.
- I think sometimes we assume others do outstanding work so we only notice or say something when they don't. Have to work on that.
- It happens, but not publicly. We have issues with this one.

In a situation where the organization failed to recognize outstanding work toward the common goal, coworkers decided to provide their own solution. The respondent explained, "Because of the spotty and inadequate efforts of top management to acknowledge workers' efforts the workers themselves have gradually taken responsibility for publicly recognizing good work, hard work, and exceptional achievements by fellow workers."

Bond Among Participants

Several people described their relationships with other organization members as those of a family: "We like to think of ourselves as a big family. And we believe it." Even a newcomer to one organization said, "We'll become family, I can feel it." The closeness of these bonds, in most cases, reflects members' dedication to their shared purpose. One respondent's comment illustrates this point: "Our team experience is very strong, despite the fact that most of us have never worked together before. We are united by the purpose of why we are here." A few companies were started by family members and close friends, and in some cases founding members are still present in the organization.

Other respondents frequently used the terms *friend* or *friendship* to describe their bonds with coworkers. For example, respondents said, "With few exceptions my colleagues ARE my friends and vice-versa," or "I have definitely made some lifelong friends among peers for whom I have a great deal of respect." Some commented that their friendship bonds existed in their immediate work unit, team, or department, and by implication, did not necessarily extend to the whole organization. Several employees stated that they were new to the organization but could see the potential for forming close bonds with members of the organization.

There were very few negative or cautionary comments regarding this topic. One respondent pointed out that working in a remote office made it difficult to develop strong relationships. Another commented that annual rotation of the leadership body did not necessarily diminish the bond among members, but it weakened aspects of management and efficiency. Another person quipped, "What can I say? I'm 100% introvert on the Myers-Briggs test!"

Self-Agency and Leadership

Our survey found that many respondents felt they and their colleagues had the power to act on behalf of their organization's common purpose. Some respondents agreed emphatically: "Most certainly," "We are always encouraged to do this," and "There are a ton of opportunities to engage and step up." Several people indicated that even the most junior workers were able to contribute their ideas: "When I started, I was in a much more junior position but I still had opportunities to impact the business every day. No one in the organization has a monopoly on good ideas."

A few respondents expressed more caution about acting solely on their own accord:

- It's hard to say, really. Oftentimes, I will have ideas and I would like to act on them. But, making a mistake could hurt everyone, so no matter how confident I am, I always like to run an idea past as many people as I can before I take it to the heads.
- I feel I have the power to act, but not always the support I need from others (mostly due to their own work pressures rather than any lack of engagement).

Some respondents explained that they were expected to check with decision-making committees or higher authorities before making certain decisions. One respondent said, "We cannot act without proper approval from certain committees, depending on what the desired action is." Different workplaces and environments generated different levels of self-agency based on organization type, structure, organizational culture, and an employee's level of experience. One respondent expressed this perspective well: "I believe this [self-agency] is a feeling that develops with time and closer connection to the organization. I would expect it to be different for different people at different levels of their experience."

We pursued the issue of self-agency more extensively in an open-ended format. We asked respondents to describe a situation in which they were inspired to take action or leadership on behalf of their organization's purpose. The situations they described varied as broadly as the organizations they represented, and individuals described situations that ranged from the mundane to the extraordinary. Some patterns emerged, however, beyond each organization's different context and the respondent's specific actions.

Many people replied that they took action or leadership on behalf of the purpose frequently. They used terms such as *daily, every day, regularly,* and *very often.* Typical comments included these:

- It's hard to pick a situation because doing this is what we do every single day on so many levels.
- Everyone in the company does this all the time. We are all leaders together.
- Every day when a coworker asks for assistance.
- Every day when I work with my clients I'm in this situation. I am often experimenting and testing different initiatives.
- Almost every day in a growth company there are opportunities to do this.

As these comments imply, organization members initiated acts of leadership for various reasons. Most often they took action to solve a problem for clients or coworkers, represent the organization or make formal and informal presentations about their organization's common purpose, initiate a new idea or innovation, assume a temporary or ongoing leadership position, or avert a crisis.

Respondents commonly used the phrase "even though" to explain that they acted or led in a capacity or situation where they typically did not have an assigned role or position:

- I have always had the drive to assist tech support members, in a way that allows them to learn and grow. This is shown almost day-to-day even though I am not in a [formal] leadership or managerial role.
- I offered to run a table for our organization at . . . a local college next week even though it means working longer hours on a week night without extra pay or extra time off.
- I took it upon myself to be a great representative of the company at our most recent customer event, even though this is well outside my comfort range and skill set.
- I took the lead on 3 such events—coordinating sponsorship, promotions, and participating in panels—even though my "day job" . . . is very demanding.

Taking Action Visibly or Invisibly

People in the survey seemed more interested in achieving the organization's common purpose than the role (leader or team member) they played in the organization. A respondent commented, "I have had the experience of both [leader and team member roles] and I enjoy both for different reasons. From either role I can feel a clear connection to the organizational purpose." Others said, "I am willing to be whatever I need to be to get things done," and "this is something we do naturally." One person summarized the relationship between one's organizational role and the common purpose aptly:

> It doesn't really matter what role you have, as long as you are capable of elevating the team in unison. And, if you can't, speak up, no one will think any less of you and we'll try and figure out another way you can help. In the end, the goal speaks for the team, not the individual.

Others expressed that they were not always comfortable with or experienced enough for a leadership role. They noted, "I've tried my hand at project management and much prefer to be a [team member]," and "due to my experience I am not always capable of acting in a leadership role. I am, however, working toward gaining more experience in this area."

Most respondents were willing to fulfill the common purpose in both visible and invisible roles, but more respondents preferred behind-the-scenes roles than visible spokesperson or organizational representative roles. Reasons for their preferences varied based on personal choice, personality, or job assignment:

- I enjoy working behind the scenes, not one for the spotlight.
- I have successfully performed as a "public face" in the past, but this is not a role that I seek or particularly enjoy.
- Not every role can be client facing or high profile and I have happily done both.
- My role is to be the "public face" of the company.

Some people said they were naturally introverted, while others were insecure about public speaking or too inexperienced to represent the organization externally.

Rising Above Self-Interest

Most respondents were willing to place the organization's common purpose above personal interests or desires when necessary and believed that their coworkers would do the same. Several respondents saw their personal interests as aligned with the common purpose, and consequently had no tension or conflict between the two factors. Their comments illustrated this perspective:

- There is such alignment that it feels to me this seldom arises.
- I think we all clearly do this, as we all could be working at higher paying organizations with less mission-based goals.
- People here do what has to be done to get the job done.

Others saw the organization's successful achievement of the common purpose as linked to their self-interest; for example, "I want the company to succeed so I can keep working here!"

Still, some respondents were reluctant to place the common purpose above their self-interest in certain instances. Some respondents expressed a need to balance their personal needs with achieving the common purpose:

- I have a life outside work.
- Sure, [I would place the purpose above my personal needs as long as] I keep having time to study and to dedicate to the organization, that's fine.
- Well, [I would be willing to place] some of them [above my personal needs].

A few respondents were not sure how to interpret the term *personal interests or desires*. One respondent said, "[It] depends on what you mean by 'personal interests and desires.' I won't compromise my needs or values in the name of any organization." Another person felt that the company left little option: "I am almost forced to place our common purpose above my personal interests or desires, when necessary."

Utilizing Opportunities and Resources

More than three-fourths of the respondents thought their organization members knew how to take advantage of opportunities and resources to advance the common purpose. Several respondents' comments illustrate how organizations grasp these opportunities using collaborative, inclusive efforts among their members:

- When we have a company-wide opportunity, be it an event, a big pitch or even raising capital, it's all hands on deck. Everyone is aware of these turning points and is clear on how to take advantage of them.
- We have a very robust recruiting process, which allows us to find the other two [financial and technological resources] after we get the human resources.
- We have a strong network of people and significant support from corporate partners and high-ranking people who advise us and connect us to the needed resources.

Several respondents acknowledged that their organizations could do better with taking advantage of opportunities and resources. They wrote, "We need to get better at this—it's complex," and "we're getting better at this." A few people lamented that members of their organization did not seize opportunities and resources:

- It pains me to say so, but I haven't seen much evidence of this: I do hope, however, that I am wrong and missing something, or that this situation will change in the near future.
- I know the desire is there, but I don't see much practical evidence to support it: I am sure we can all get better at this!

A small number of respondents indicated that they did not know or were unsure if their organization knew how to make use of opportunities and resources: "I think this [my organization takes advantage of opportunities and resources] is probably true but I'm really not sure."

Overall, these robust comments from our respondents provide vital insight into how invisible leadership functions in companies and nonprofits, and reveal examples of practices or processes that work well or need improvement. Their perspectives and responses give us a starting point for creating and sustaining leadership in organizations with varied purposes and diverse contexts. In the next chapter, we will use these insights along with our survey data to discuss possible ways practitioners and researchers could benefit from this initial study.

6

Leading Invisibly

The Common Purpose as Leader

Invisible leadership, as we defined it in Chapter 1, embodies situations in which *dedication to a compelling and deeply held common purpose* is the motivating force for leadership. This common purpose provides the inspiration for participants to use their strengths willingly in leader or follower roles and cultivates a strong shared bond that connects participants to each other in pursuit of the purpose.

Our survey of award-winning companies suggests that invisible leadership has relevance for both the study and the practice of leadership. We offer some guidance for implementing invisible leadership based on the advice and comments from our participants recorded in Chapter 5, and we pose questions that we hope will stimulate further research. We begin with the possibilities for practice and end with potential paths for future research.

Invisible Leadership: Possibilities for Practice

Create the Context

It may seem that we have developed a case for eliminating the role of positional leader. Quite the contrary, our study participants conveyed to us that leaders have a vital and distinctive role in invisible leadership. Their first and most essential role is to create an environment where the common purpose leads *and* people thrive. In this context, leaders "facilitate the work" of a group or organization; they do not control or take possession of it. As acknowledged by Lao Tzu, "The wise leader does not intervene unnecessarily. The leader's presence is felt, but often the group runs itself" (Heider, 1985, p. 33).

Leaders make certain that the common purpose maintains prominence in all actions, from hiring to finance to fun. They strive to embody the essence of the common purpose and model ethical, open, and caring behavior. They cultivate a context where purpose is a lived experience among members of the organization. This organizational environment fosters collective capacity, facilitates selection of new members, engages members in meaningful work, facilitates a strong bond or relationship among employees, supports role flexibility, and facilitates change (see Figure 6.1).

> "Interacting with senior leadership [SLT] and having the SLT reiterate and live the purpose transparently is by far one of the biggest influences on me personally. I've worked in companies where the leadership is a mysterious shadow looming in some high-floor office, never seen or heard from directly. What will make [this organization] great is the SLT's involvement in the culture and the day to day."

Cultivate Purpose as Lived Experience

Members willingly undertake the common purpose, while leaders cultivate a context where members engage in ongoing dialogue about the purpose through conversations, forums, teams, and other formats. Leaders and members ask each other, What is it about our work, our relationships, and our organization that makes us valuable, unique, or significant? How do we communicate the significance of our purpose to members and people outside the organization? Is our purpose ethical—that is, does it protect one person's individual rights and needs against and alongside the rights and needs of others? Do we live the purpose daily and use it ethically as the guiding light for all decisions and processes? How do we hold ourselves accountable for keeping the purpose at the center of our work? Obviously, the answers to these questions vary in each organization. The role of leaders is to keep these and other questions at the forefront of the organization and to develop processes to ensure that they and their members address them on a

> "Our strong sense of purpose—our mission—gives us all something to return to and focus on when the day-to-day work of running a company, making profit and dealing with tricky client issues, can otherwise leave some people fighting to see the woods from the trees. It helps us understand how our work contributes to a 'higher purpose' and plays an enormous part in bringing us all together in pursuit of something bigger than ourselves."

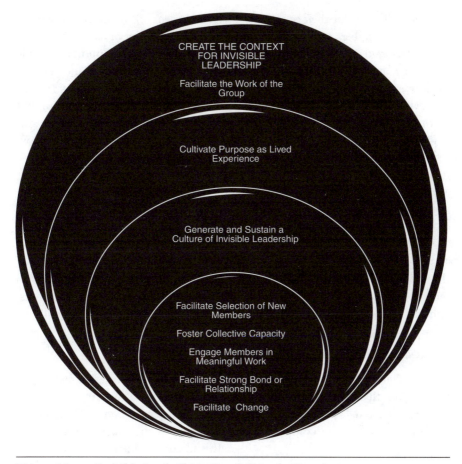

Figure 6.1   Invisible Leadership—Possibilities for Practice

consistent basis. How can organizations facilitate a discussion of these issues? One survey participant described leaders who scheduled and conducted regular reviews and dialogues to constantly reconnect employees with their purpose and link it to the work they perform. Each organization can develop a process that meets the unique needs of its purpose and members to address these questions on a regular basis.

Generate and Sustain a Culture of Invisible Leadership

Leaders and members develop and sustain an ethical culture of inclusion, participation, and transparency where all people are valued and respected. They believe in the substance and capability of their people and the organization where they work. They value their organization's environment of trust and care, because leaders and members foster the development and well-being of each other.

Leaders and members cultivate workplace design that supports invisible leadership and allows people to participate in the organization and interact freely with coworkers at all levels across teams, departments, organizations, and cyberspace to accomplish the common purpose. This does not mean that all organizations must become democratic organizations like those in the survey. It does mean that invisible leadership flourishes where work designs allow members to generate new approaches, solve problems, and fully use their intellect and creativity to accomplish the common purpose. Specifically, we suggest that the role of leaders in generating and sustaining a culture of invisible leadership is to facilitate the selection of new members, foster collective capacity, engage members in meaningful work, facilitate a strong bond or relationship among members, and facilitate change. We discuss each of these responsibilities individually.

> "I have worked at many companies large and small over the years, and I have never worked at a company that had integrity, honesty, and openness more woven into the fabric of its being."

Facilitate Selection of New Members

No other process is more important to sustaining a lived commitment to the purpose than selecting new members for the organization. As one respondent emphasized, "Rigorous hiring ensures that nearly everyone on board is very engaged in the company." Commitment to the purpose means that new and current members embrace the purpose as they simultaneously engage in contributing their ideas and diverse perspectives. Leaders ensure that these factors are emphasized and that team members participate fully in the selection process. One company uses a screening process it calls "mission match," where it assesses new members to determine whether their stated passion, interest, or work history show compatibility with the common purpose.

> "We attract and carefully screen potential staff members on what we call mission match to make sure that we hire folks who really care about our mission."

After new members join the organization, some companies and nonprofits conduct classes to induct individuals into the organization, fully communicate its purpose and culture, and provide training on jobs or roles in the organization. Zappos, an online retail company on the Worldblu Most Democratic Companies list, provides classes for all new employees where they learn about the company and commit to its 10 core values:

1. Deliver WOW Through Service

2. Embrace and Drive Change

3. Create Fun and a Little Weirdness

4. Be Adventurous, Creative, and Open-Minded

5. Pursue Growth and Learning

6. Build Open and Honest Relationships With Communication

7. Build a Positive Team and Family Spirit

8. Do More With Less

9. Be Passionate and Determined

10. Be Humble (Zappos, n.d.)

Before their graduation ceremony, the company offers new members money to walk away if they are not passionate about the Zappos purpose and culture.

A key focus of the selection process is to choose new colleagues who embrace the purpose while infusing the organization with innovative ways of approaching problems, products, or services. As one respondent commented, "Everyone, especially new folks, is encouraged to take action to improve our methods and their execution." The leader's role is to provide a context in which new and continuing members can be simultaneously committed to the purpose and engage in free expression of ideas or dissent. Leaders and members demonstrate in team meetings, discussions, brainstorming, planning sessions, and other group settings that open, honest comments and perspectives are valued and receive full consideration. As discussed in Chapter 3, they establish practices of limiting premature seeking of concurrence, correcting misperceptions and biases, and using effective decision-making techniques.

Foster Collective Capacity

Collective capacity (or the increased competency of a group over each of its members acting alone) involves members contributing their best efforts to the shared work of the group. Leaders and members can foster collective capacity by working in pairs or teams, learning and training for multiple roles or jobs, and providing opportunities for teams and individuals to develop professionally and personally. Using these shared approaches to the work of a company or nonprofit can develop collective capacity by helping members understand the organization beyond the limits of their individual

"We form the best integrated team I've ever seen: Developers, testers, business analysts, and project managers all WORK TOGETHER!!!"

position or team. As a result, members exercise self-agency by thinking and acting with a more informed perspective. Leaders and members strengthen collective capacity when they are encouraged to take on roles and responsibilities that get the work done regardless of official roles or the visibility of their efforts. They can encourage self-agency in members to act on behalf of collective aims, and recognize admirable team work.

As we indicated in Chapter 5, our respondents said they exercise self-agency outside their regular roles or positions most often to solve a problem for clients or coworkers, represent the organization or make presentations about the common purpose, initiate a new idea or innovation, assume a leadership role, or avert a crisis.

"We are ever learning and training ourselves to learn new courses and acquire certifications."

They cautioned that exercising self-agency entails a combination of personal experience in the organization, understanding what needs to be done, knowing when you need guidance or consent from others, willingness to help, and the initiative and courage to act. They advise members to consider these factors even when they are explicitly encouraged to act by team members or leaders.

Engage Members in Meaningful Work

Leaders and members engage people throughout the organization in meaningful work, according to our survey respondents. Philosopher Joanne Ciulla (2000) explains that "Meaningful work, like a meaningful life, is morally worthy work undertaken in a morally worthy organization. Work has meaning *because* there is some good in it" (p. 225). This meaning, according to Ciulla, makes life better for others or creates products that help people.

People in our invisible leadership study expressed a passion for being engaged in meaningful work. Leaders and members can draw on several interrelated factors to create meaningful work in their organizations—the common purpose, development of collective capacity, and role flexibility. When members maintain focus on an inspiring purpose, they contribute their talents and competencies because they believe in the value and benefit of the organization's purpose.

Invisible leadership provides one of the strongest incentives for people to join and continue in an organization—that is, dedication to a compelling and deeply held common purpose. Its emphasis on intrinsic motivation (inspiration generated internally by an individual) facilitates meaningful work. Members of most organizations in the survey indicated that their organization's compelling common purpose and the work that accompanied it inspired them to contribute their best effort. They were also influenced by opportunities for professional growth and career development, a highly participative environment, and supportive, committed team members. Leaders facilitated the meaningful work of each group, making certain that people understood why their work mattered to the common purpose, and providing opportunities for individuals and teams to develop their abilities.

> "It's fantastic because we can see the change every day when looking at the people our product touches. I hear it from my personal networks who work at the companies we work with. It makes the desire to succeed and continue to spread our great platform that much stronger."

There are also extrinsic motivations (incentives generated or granted by others) that contribute to meaningful work. Several organizations in the study developed formal and informal approaches to recognize and reward coworkers. Some acknowledge each other for outstanding work toward achieving the purpose by voting for the top five contributors to the team's work, openly acknowledging them, and providing an added bonus. Other groups confer monthly "awesome" awards, cheer for team members who achieve a win, provide positive informal feedback, or recognize coworkers' contributions publicly.

Most notably, respondents commented that recognition and rewards acknowledge collective work or team members' contributions to the work of the group. They were less focused on individual reward systems. The role of leaders in this process is to foster and support formal and informal recognition and rewards that are most relevant to the teams and people in the organization, and, as one person commented, create a daily environment of positive reinforcement. They should make certain that these incentives are a vital component of the organization's culture.

Facilitate a Strong Bond or Relationship Among Members

Our participants explained that strong bonds of relationship, friendship, cooperation, and trust develop in environments where commitment to the common purpose is a daily lived experience. Members willingly bring their capabilities to the work, and leaders create contexts where purpose and people thrive. These strong bonds or relationships in invisible leadership are like the blue notes in jazz described in Chapter 1—the powerful yet invisible relationship

> "We have ended up feeling like family you get to choose—the people who we hire are those we feel most comfortable sharing a large portion of our waking hours with and by treating each other well we end up with very loyal and hard-working employees."

between notes makes the music soar. In the same way, these strong bonds forged by a convergence of the common purpose, collective work toward the purpose, and creation of trusting and cooperative relationships form the "power" of invisible leadership. To facilitate this convergence, leaders play a supporting role to the group. They keep the common purpose in the forefront, sustain the link to meaningful work, provide optimal work spaces or technology that enable maximum interaction and teamwork, invigorate the culture with work and social rituals or celebrations, provide professional development, and attend to the well-being of members.

Facilitate Change

Change is constant in invisible leadership cultures as in any organization. Leaders and members must remain true to the culture of inclusion, participation, transparency, trust, and care in bringing about organizational change, especially change that involves altering the purpose itself. Several respondents warned of the problems that ensue when leaders implement change without regard for these critical factors.

The role of leaders is to establish decision-making processes that are consistent with invisible leadership—open, inclusive, and guided by common purpose. These processes require member involvement before choices are made about organizational change. This does not mean that every member must agree or vote on every change. Some processes may be as simple as agreeing to use consensus decision making and vote only in cases where full consensus cannot be reached. Other processes may use representatives elected by teams, units, or departments and a process of discussion and voting to make final decisions. These processes should also specify how decision making should proceed in crisis or emergency situations.

Generating Scholarship: Possibilities for Research on Invisible Leadership

We believe that the power of a compelling common purpose can generate leadership in various contexts—companies, nonprofit organizations, communities, public service, and social movements. Our research identified several interconnected factors that compose invisible leadership (see Figure 6.2).

There is much more work to be done and many questions to explore. We included our research results and survey instrument in the hope that future studies will use and refine the factors, scales, and measures in our

Figure 6.2   Interrelated Factors in Invisible Leadership

survey; identify and address further ethical issues and pitfalls that leaders and members must confront; and tackle questions still unanswered by this initial research. We raise several questions for future study: Does invisible leadership vary in different contexts such as public agencies, corporations, or social movements? How does organization design or structure (team based, virtual, bureaucratic, or democratic) affect invisible leadership? Can invisible leadership be sustained over long periods of time? Does the composition or diversity of a group affect invisible leadership? What effect does organization or group size have on invisible leadership?

Our initial work demonstrates that people and organizations benefit when common purpose is the invisible leader. We hope you will join us in continuing this work. This new look at leadership will impact how we experience and understand the organizations and movements of the future—from innovative companies and nonprofits, such as the WorldBlu award winners, to large movements like the Arab Spring.

References

Ciulla, J. B. (2000). *The working life: The promise and betrayal of modern work*. New York, NY: Times Books.

Heider, J. L. (1985). *The tao of leadership: Lao Tzu's tao te ching adapted for a new age*. Atlanta, GA: Humanics New Age.

Zappos. (n.d.). *Zappos family core values*. Retrieved August 22, 2012, from http://about.zappos.com/our-unique-culture/zappos-core-values

Appendix

Invisible Leadership Survey

Questions

This survey focuses on your view of your organization's purpose, where

1. *organization* refers to your work unit—the group of people you work with most directly, and

2. *purpose* or *common purpose* refers to the organization's basic reason for existing, including its mission and multiple bottom lines.

Please check the best response to each question.

1. The main reason I joined my organization is its

___ Compensation (pay and/or benefits).

___ Purpose.

___ Brand or reputation.

___ Location (proximity) to my home.

___ Team members or coworkers.

___ Work environment.

___ Professional growth or career opportunities.

___ Job security.

___ Job opening/available position.

___ Other (please specify) _____

2. The main reason I stay at my organization is its

___ Compensation (pay and/or benefits).

___ Purpose.

___ Brand or reputation.

___ Location (proximity) to my home.

___ Team members or coworkers.

___ Work environment.

___ Professional growth or career opportunities.

___ Job security.

___ Job opening/available position.

___ Other (please specify) _____

3. Please describe your organization's purpose.

_____

_____

_____

4. I am highly committed to achieving my organization's purpose.

___ Strongly disagree

___ Disagree

___ Somewhat disagree

___ Neutral

___ Somewhat agree

___ Agree

___ Strongly agree

Comments:

_____

_____

_____

5. My coworkers accept the organization's purpose as their own.

___ Strongly disagree

___ Disagree

___ Somewhat disagree

___ Neutral

___ Somewhat agree

___ Agree

___ Strongly agree

___ I don't know

Comments:

_____

_____

_____

6. I accept the organization's purpose as my own.

___ Strongly disagree

___ Disagree

___ Somewhat disagree

___ Neutral

___ Somewhat agree

___ Agree

Comments:

_____

_____

_____

7. The organization's purpose reflects my personal passion.

___ Strongly disagree

___ Disagree

___ Somewhat disagree

___ Neutral

___ Somewhat agree

___ Agree

___ Strongly agree

Comments:

_____

_____

_____

8. My organization's purpose inspires me to contribute my best effort or work.

___ Strongly disagree

___ Disagree

___ Somewhat disagree

___ Neutral

___ Somewhat agree

___ Agree

___ Strongly agree

Comments:

_____

_____

_____

9. My organization's purpose inspires my coworkers to contribute their best effort or work.

___ Strongly disagree

___ Disagree

___ Somewhat disagree

___ Neutral

___ Somewhat agree

___ Agree

___ Strongly agree

___ I don't know

Comments:

_____

_____

_____

10. My organization acknowledges individuals for outstanding work toward achieving the purpose.

___ Strongly disagree

___ Disagree

___ Somewhat disagree

___ Neutral

___ Somewhat agree

___ Agree

___ Strongly agree

Comments:

_____

_____

_____

11. Members of my organization recognize or praise each other for outstanding work toward achieving the purpose.

___ Strongly disagree

___ Disagree

___ Somewhat disagree

___ Neutral

___ Somewhat agree

___ Agree

___ Strongly agree

___ I don't know

Comments:

_____

_____

_____

12. Our work toward the organization's purpose creates a strong bond or relationship among its members.

___ Strongly disagree

___ Disagree

___ Somewhat disagree

___ Neutral

___ Somewhat agree

___ Agree

___ Strongly agree

Comments:

_____

_____

_____

13. I have a strong bond or relationship with members of my organization.

___ Strongly disagree

___ Disagree

___ Somewhat disagree

___ Neutral

___ Somewhat agree

___ Agree

___ Strongly agree

Comments:

_____

_____

_____

14. I feel I have the power to act on behalf of my organization's purpose.

___ Strongly disagree

___ Disagree

___ Somewhat disagree

___ Neutral

___ Somewhat agree

___ Agree

___ Strongly agree

Comments:

_____

_____

_____

15. Most members of my organization feel they have the power to act on behalf of our purpose.

___ Strongly disagree

___ Disagree

___ Somewhat disagree

___ Neutral

___ Somewhat agree

___ Agree

___ Strongly agree

___ I don't know

Comments:

_____

_____

_____

16. I am willing to work in either a leader or team member role to reach the organization's common goal.

___ Strongly disagree

___ Disagree

___ Somewhat disagree

___ Neutral

___ Somewhat agree

___ Agree

___ Strongly agree

Comments:

_____

_____

_____

17. I am willing to work in a role that is not visible to people outside my organization to achieve my organization's purpose.

___ Strongly disagree

___ Disagree

___ Somewhat disagree

___ Neutral

___ Somewhat agree

___ Agree

___ Strongly agree

Comments:

_____

_____

_____

18. I am willing to work in a visible role as a spokesperson or representative to achieve my organization's purpose.

___ Strongly disagree

___ Disagree

___ Somewhat disagree

___ Neutral

___ Somewhat agree

___ Agree

___ Strongly agree

Comments:

_____

_____

_____

19. I place our common purpose above my personal interests or desires, when necessary.

___ Strongly disagree

___ Disagree

___ Somewhat disagree

___ Neutral

___ Somewhat agree

___ Agree

___ Strongly agree

Comments:

_____

_____

_____

20. My coworkers place our common purpose above their personal interests or desires, when necessary.

___ Strongly disagree

___ Disagree

___ Somewhat disagree

___ Neutral

___ Somewhat agree

___ Agree

___ Strongly agree

___ I don't know

Comments:

_____

_____

_____

21. My coworkers know how or when to make use of key opportunities (occasions, decisive moments, turning points) that make achieving our common purpose possible.

___ Strongly disagree

___ Disagree

___ Somewhat disagree

___ Neutral

___ Somewhat agree

___ Agree

___ Strongly agree

___ I don't know

Comments:

_____

_____

_____

22. My coworkers know how to find resources (financial, human, or technological) that make achieving our common purpose possible.

___ Strongly disagree

___ Disagree

___ Somewhat disagree

___ Neutral

___ Somewhat agree

____ Agree

____ Strongly agree

____ I don't know

Comments:

_____

_____

_____

23. Please describe a situation in which you were inspired to take action or leadership on behalf of your organization's purpose.

_____

_____

_____

24. Additional comments about the influence of your organization's purpose on you or your coworkers:

_____

_____

_____

Demographic Information

25. Name of your organization or company?

_____

_____

_____

26. Sector:

____ Business/corporation

____ Nonprofit/nongovernmental organization

____ Government

____ Education (K–12)

____ Higher education

____ B corporation

____ Other (please specify) _____

27. Which category best describes your connection to the organization or company?

___ Employee/team member/staff member

___ Faculty member/instructor

___ Manager/supervisor/team leader

___ Executive/senior manager/senior leader

___ Other (please specify) _____

28. I am a

___ Full-time employee

___ Part-time employee

___ Volunteer

___ Retiree or emeritus member

___ Other (please specify) _____

29. How many years have you been employed by this organization?

_____

_____

_____

30. I am a

___ Male

___ Female

31. My age (in years)

_____

_____

_____

Researchers may use this survey free of charge with the proper citation of this text. Please let us know of your results.

Index

About the Authors

Dr. Gill Robinson Hickman is currently professor emerita in the Jepson School of Leadership Studies at the University of Richmond. She was an inaugural faculty member of the Jepson School and participated in its institution building and course development. Hickman has held positions as dean, professor of public administration, and human resource director. She has published several books, including *Leading Change in Multiple Contexts: Concepts and Practices in Organizational, Community, Political, Social, and Global Change Settings; Leading Organizations: Perspectives for a New Era* (1st and 2nd editions); and *Managing Personnel in the Public Sector: A Shared Responsibility,* with Dalton Lee. She also published numerous articles and book chapters in the field of leadership studies.

Her experience has led to invitations to present at the China Executive Leadership Academy Pudong (CELAP), Shanghai, China, and at the Leadership in Central Europe Conference at Palacky University in Olomouc, Czech Republic, and to be a panel member at international conferences in Amsterdam, The Netherlands; Guadalajara, Mexico; and Vancouver and Toronto, Canada. She was also a faculty presenter at the prestigious Salzburg Seminar in Salzburg, Austria, and at the University of the Western Cape in South Africa, where she presented a conceptual framework for leadership and transformation for regional governments in South Africa. Hickman served as vice president and board member of the International Leadership Association and participates annually in its conference as a panel member or chair. She has used her expertise over the years to advise countless leadership studies programs nationally and internationally. E-mail contact: ghickman@richmond.edu.

Dr. Georgia J. Sorenson envisioned and launched the James MacGregor Burns Academy of Leadership at the University of Maryland—the first academic program devoted to public leadership—more than 20 years ago. She is cofounder of the International Leadership Association (with Larraine

Matusak and James MacGregor Burns). Currently she is visiting professor of leadership studies at the Carey School of Law at the University of Maryland. She has served as a board member of the Leadership Learning Community, the Kellogg Fellows Leadership Alliance, the Academy for Educational Development's New Voices, the Asian Pacific American Women's Leadership Institute, Learning to Lead, and many other leadership organizations in the United States and abroad. Sorenson is the author of several books, including *Dead Center: Clinton–Gore Leadership and the Perils of Moderation* with James MacGregor Burns, published in 1999 by Scribner. Sorenson is coeditor, with George R. Goethals and James MacGregor Burns, of the four-volume *Encyclopedia of Leadership,* published by SAGE in 2004. She has published in professional journals, such as the *Harvard Educational Review, Signs,* and *Psychology of Women Quarterly,* and is a frequent contributor to and commentator on leadership and social issues in the popular media.

Sorenson's experience has led to numerous international consultancies and teaching appointments. She was adjunct professor at Ewha Womans University in Seoul, Korea; serves as professor and adviser to China's National School of Administration; and was on the international board of the Tokyo Jogakkan College in Japan. Previously she served on the advisory board of the Thierry Graduate School of Leadership. Before launching her career in academia, Sorenson was a senior policy analyst for employment issues in the Carter White House and later worked as a consultant to the Executive Office of the President. During her White House tenure, she served on the White House Productivity Council and on Vice President Walter Mondale's Youth Employment Council. She continues to be politically active and has served as a speechwriter or consultant to three presidential campaigns. E-mail contact: gsorenson@law.umaryland.edu.

⑤SAGE researchmethods

The essential online tool for researchers from the world's leading methods publisher

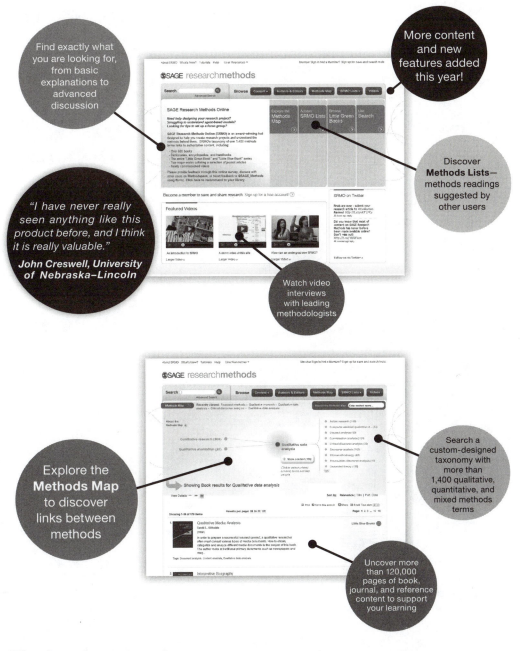

Find exactly what you are looking for, from basic explanations to advanced discussion

More content and new features added this year!

Discover **Methods Lists**— methods readings suggested by other users

"I have never really seen anything like this product before, and I think it is really valuable."

John Creswell, University of Nebraska–Lincoln

Watch video interviews with leading methodologists

Explore the **Methods Map** to discover links between methods

Search a custom-designed taxonomy with more than 1,400 qualitative, quantitative, and mixed methods terms

Uncover more than 120,000 pages of book, journal, and reference content to support your learning

Find out more at
www.sageresearchmethods.com